GOSPEL HOPE
for Sexual Sin and Brokenness
IN MARRIAGE

KRISTYN PEREZ

Gospel Hope for Sexual Sin and Brokenness in Marriage
Copyright © 2023 by The Daily Grace Co.®
Spring, Texas. All rights reserved.

Unless otherwise noted, all Scripture quotations are taken from the Christian Standard Bible®, Copyright © 2020 by Holman Bible Publishers. Used by permission. Christian Standard Bible® and CSB® are federally registered trademarks of Holman Bible Publishers.

The extra on page 100 is from *Worthy: Embracing Your Identity in Christ*. Copyright © 2022 by the Daily Grace Co.® Learn more about this resource on page 110.

The Daily Grace Co.® exists to equip disciples to know and love God and His Word by creating beautiful, theologically rich, and accessible resources so that God may be glorified and the gospel made known.

Any italicized text in Scripture quotations is the author's own emphasis.

Designed in the United States of America and printed in China.

In this resource

1: GOD'S DESIGN FOR SEXUALITY — 4

2: THE PROBLEM — 16

3: PORNOGRAPHY AND MASTURBATION — 24

4: PURITY IN MARRIAGE — 52

5: ABUSE — 70

6: HOMOSEXUALITY AND TRANSGENDERISM — 78

7: DIFFICULT EMOTIONS AND SEXUALITY — 90

8: THE HOPE OF THE GOSPEL — 104

CHAPTER ONE

God's Design for Sexuality

IN THIS CHAPTER

An Introduction
The Hope of God's Word
God and Sexuality

God's Design for Gender
God's Design for Marriage
God's Design for Sex

Jesus came to redeem and restore all things, even our sexuality.

01 / God's Design for Sexuality

God's Design for Sexuality: An Introduction

God cares about your sexuality. Does that thought make you cringe? Do you feel embarrassed by the mention of the word "sex" or judged by God because of sexual sin? Do you feel stifled, confused, or hopeless, wondering if your sexual life will ever feel satisfying or whole?

For many, the idea that God cares about their sex lives is a foreign concept, confusing and jarring. Brokenness, pain, and abuse have tainted God's good gift of sex. Culture has elevated sexual freedom as a human right, leaving many feeling confused, discouraged, or dirty. But thankfully, there is healing and hope offered to all through the gospel of Jesus Christ. Jesus came to redeem and restore all things, even our sexuality.

From the beginning of mankind, God planned for sex, gender, and sexuality to be a part of His good design, tangible reflections of His covenantal love and perfect character (Genesis 2:18, 23–24). Although sex has been distorted, abused, and manipulated throughout history, God created it as a gift. He designed sex to be a blessing enjoyed between husband and wife within the confines of marriage, and He desires for our marriages to be filled with intimacy, joy, and love (Proverbs 5:19, Song of Songs 5:1).

Throughout this booklet, we will be discussing God's design for sexuality, marriage, and gender. We will discuss common sources of sexual sin, such as pornography, masturbation, and lust, and we will discover the hope of the gospel for sexual sin and shame. We will also provide practical help and resources for each topic. It is important to note that throughout this booklet, we will discuss God's design for sex and sexuality primarily within the context of marriage. For an in-depth look at sex and sexuality as it relates to singleness, see *Gospel Hope in Sexuality and Singleness,* which you can purchase at www.thedailygraceco.com.

Regardless of your sexual past or current struggles, remember: God is a God of forgiveness, healing, and hope. He can redeem every sinful thought and action. He can remove every shame. He can be trusted, and His plans for you are good.

The Hope of God's Word

The Bible contains all we need for life and godliness, even as it relates to our sexuality. Therefore, throughout this booklet, we will study God's Word to uncover His design for sex and sexuality. As we study this topic throughout this booklet, four primary truths will guide our approach:

God is good.

God is the satisfaction for our deepest longings. He designed sex as a gift that points us to His goodness. He gives us good gifts, not so that they will become an end in themselves but rather so that they will be a reflection of His love and goodness.

God's plans are good.

When God places limitations on our sexual lives or expression, it is not to hurt us. Rather, it is for our good.

God forgives and restores.

There is no sexual sin that is beyond forgiveness. There is no sexual brokenness that is beyond God's healing. He desires for you to have freedom from sexual sin and healing from sexual hurt. There is hope for sexual sin and brokenness.

The Spirit of God empowers us to live holy lives.

When we trust in Jesus, God gives us His Spirit to live inside us. We are set apart and made holy for His glory. God doesn't leave us to our own devices but empowers us to live righteous lives. He changes us, purifies us, and transforms us so that we can be holy.

Before we continue, it is important to define the word "gospel." As Christians, the gospel is the foundation of our lives. It defines our hope, our purpose, and how we are made right with God.

The gospel is the following message: We were all separated from a holy God because of our sins, unable to save ourselves. Because of our sins, we each stood guilty before our Maker, condemned to eternal death. But thankfully, God didn't leave us this way. He sent His only Son, Jesus, into the world to enter our brokenness and do what we could not do on our own. Jesus lived a perfect life, thus fulfilling the Law's demands, and died a substitutionary death on the cross, taking our sins upon Himself and offering us His righteousness through faith. Because of the gospel, we are free from sin and shame and made right with God. We can have hope for freedom from sexual sin and shame because Christ has set us free, paying our once-and-for-all sacrifice on the cross. He has made us new and has given us His Holy Spirit to live within us, convicting us of sin and empowering us to live godly lives.

In summary, the gospel message is this: God sent His Son, Jesus, to save sinners by dying for their sins on the cross and rising again from the grave. All who repent of their sins and confess that Christ is Lord will be saved. This is the good news that changes everything.

God and Sexuality: Evaluating Your Views about Sex

What do you think about sex?

Many Christians view their sexuality as disconnected from their faith, a conglomeration of private decisions and experiences to be had apart from the wisdom of God's Word and the discipleship of other believers. Years of experiences, images, conversations, and sin lead them to believe their sexuality is unrelated to their Christian lives. They consider sexuality as *private* and subconsciously conclude that God doesn't care about that part of their lives.

For many who grew up in conservative circles, sex was taught as a secret mystery reserved only for marriage. They were told not to think about sex before marriage, but after the wedding, they were expected to flip the proverbial switch and become sexual experts overnight. For others, they were taught that sexual desire was the equivalent of any other physical need—a pleasure that must be satisfied freely and without limitations.

Furthermore, compartmentalizing sexual sins is compounded by the feeling that Christians cannot talk about sexual struggles. Within the church, many may feel comfortable confessing the "safe" sins of impatience or pride, but what about their pornography addictions? Would many married women feel safe confessing lust toward a co-worker as a prayer request in a Bible study group?

Take a moment to consider your views about sex and sexuality. Do you view sex as a private exchange between two consenting adults? Or do you view it as a dirty source of pain because of past trauma? Has your view of sex been tainted by the brokenness and sin of this world, or do you view it as a beautiful gift from God? Using the space below, process your current thoughts about sex and sexuality. What people, circumstances, or resources have informed these views?

_____
_____
_____
_____
_____
_____
_____
_____
_____
_____

Compartmentalizing sexual sins is compounded by the feeling that Christians cannot talk about sexual struggles.

01: God's Design for Sexuality

God's Design for Gender

"It's a boy!" For thousands of years, one's biological sex was the primary determiner of his or her gender. There was little debate around the topic. In the hospital, babies were welcomed into the world by doctors and nurses with pink and blue signs that clearly announced, "It's a boy!" or "It's a girl!" A baby's chromosomes and physical anatomy were the universal criteria for knowing whether a child was male or female.

But in today's culture, many define gender not based on one's biology but based on how one identifies internally. This has expanded the language of gender to include a plethora of terms, such as:

- *Agender* – someone who does not identify as any gender
- *Nonbinary* – one who identifies with both the male and female gender, often fluctuating between the two
- *Gender fluid* – someone who does not permanently associate with any gender
- *Gender expansive* – one who presses against societal norms regarding gender
- *Gender questioning* – one who is questioning or exploring their gender preferences
- *Transgender* – one who feels that their gender identity does not match their biological gender

Similarly, gender pronouns are no longer limited to "he" and "she." The list now includes ze, hir, xe, xem, they, them, and zim, to name a few. So what does God's Word have to say about gender?

When God created the world, He made Adam and Eve male and female (Genesis 1:27). He designed two genders, who were created in His image and for His glory. He thoughtfully, sovereignly, and carefully made Adam and Eve and called them good. He told them to be fruitful and multiply, and they had children who were boys and girls.

In the Bible, God associates one's biological sex with his or her gender. There is no biblical example of a man believing he is a woman or a woman believing she is a man in Scripture. Instead, throughout the Bible, heroes of the faith—such as Abraham and Sarah, Isaac and Rebecca, Jeremiah, Mary, and Jesus—were born and lived their lives in alignment with their biological sex. Similarly, the Bible's commands were written to two genders, men and women, for thousands of years. The Scriptures often include specific instructions divided out by gender, and the Scriptures only reference two genders (1 Corinthians 11:8–11, Ephesians 5:22–33, 1 Timothy 2:8–15, Titus 2:3–6).

While this is God's design for gender, for many, the gender conversation is not simply an abstract or intellectual argument. We have friends or family members who are questioning their gender identities. We have children who have completed hormone therapy or are considering transitioning from one gender to another. In later sections of this booklet, we will aim to discuss these topics in a compassionate and honoring way. At the same time, it is important to remember that God designed the genders of male and female according to His good plan. He designed us to be His image-bearers as men or women, and through Scripture, we see that gender is not primarily a social construct. Sex, gender, and sexuality are parts of God's good design.

> **God designed the genders of male and female according to His good plan. He designed us to be His image-bearers as men or women, and through Scripture, we see that gender is not primarily a social construct. Sex, gender, and sexuality are parts of God's good design.**

God's Design for Marriage

Given that this booklet is designed for married women, it is likely that you know all about married life. You know the joys of marriage, of being known and loved. At the same time, you know the pain of being disappointed and hurt by your husband. As a wife, you are married to another sinner and have likely experienced the beauty and pain of relational sin.

Depending on your background, you may have dreamed of being a wife since you were a child. You longed to be a mom, to cook dinners for your husband, and to nurture your children. Perhaps you find great fulfillment in the role of "wife" and thrive in this season of life. Or maybe you are on the other end of the spectrum of women who never expected to get married. You are independent and strong and never dreamed of limiting your potential by tying the knot. Being married has been an adjustment of expectations, either as a delightful surprise or as a crash course into the reality of being married to a fellow sinner. In either case, you are currently seeing the joys and sorrows of marriage in your daily life.

Marriage was created by God and designed to be a covenant of love, commitment, and unity between husband and wife. God made marriage in the garden of Eden after creating Adam. He said that "it is not good for the man to be alone" (Genesis 2:18), and He created Eve from Adam's rib and called her Adam's wife (Genesis 2:21–23). God made Eve to be a helper to Adam and instructed that through marriage, a man would leave his father and mother to become one flesh with his wife (Genesis 2:24).

The gift of marriage was designed to point us to the covenant love of God (Ephesians 5:22–32). God created marriage as a tangible expression of His care and love, and God desires that our marriages be full of life, love, and joy as we serve one another out of reverence for Christ. Not only this, but through marriage, we were given the special gift of intimacy in the forms of emotional, spiritual, and physical closeness. Scripture declares that the marriage bed is to be honored by all, protected as pure and sacred (Hebrews 13:4). God created marriage to reveal His constant love for us through Christ.

All that being said, it is worth noting that while this is God's design, because of the Fall, sin and brokenness often invade our relationships. Although we will not have perfect marriages because of sin, we can have great marriages by God's grace. There is hope for even the hardest of marriages because of God's mighty grace and power. Later in this booklet, we will look specifically at many common problems in marriages, such as pornography, lack of intimacy, and lack of attraction between spouses. We will also review common arguments for a biblical interpretation of same-sex marriages.

The gift of marriage was designed to point us to the covenant love of God.

God's Design for Sex

God created our sexuality. He created sex as a beautiful gift to be enjoyed within marriage and desires for us to have beautiful intimacy within our marriages. He designed our sex hormones and organs. He created puberty, ovulation cycles, and sexual desire. He created sex and gave it several purposes, including unity within marriage, pleasure, procreation, and gospel illumination.

Unity

Sex is an expression of unity and oneness in marriage. As husband and wife come together as one flesh, they are called to honor one another in love. Sex is designed as a physical reaffirmation of the marital covenant to be enjoyed as two become one.

Pleasure

God created sex to be an enjoyable gift within marriage. Interestingly, there is even an entire book of the Bible (Song of Songs) dedicated to the topic of intimacy within marriage. God is not anti-pleasure or anti-sex. Instead, He is the very Author and Creator of sexual pleasure.

Procreation

When God gave Adam and Eve the command to "be fruitful and multiply," He enabled them to fulfill this command through His good gift of sex (Genesis 1:28). Children are a blessing and are created through sex.

Gospel Illumination

During sex, husband and wife are naked and vulnerable with one another. They are seen, known, and loved by their lover. As such, sex within marriage can serve as a physical reminder of not just the intimacy between a husband and a wife but the intimacy that believers now have with God. Through Christ, we are fully known, seen, and loved by our Maker.

Although God's designs for sex are good, sin often corrupts sex within marriage. Instead of being known and loved, mutually honoring one another through sexual love, sex is hard. Selfishness reigns. Disunity, division, and disdain fuel brokenness and hurt. Infertility grieves men and women who desire children. Gospel illumination is replaced with pain and loneliness. But there is hope. God is a God of healing and restoration, and He can redeem not only your soul but your entire life, including your sex and sexuality. God brings hope and purpose to our sexuality, even when it is distorted by sin. He redeems and restores all things.

"

God is a God of healing and restoration, and He can redeem not only your soul but your entire life.

GOD BRINGS HOPE AND
PURPOSE TO OUR SEXUALITY,

even when it is distorted by sin.

HE REDEEMS AND
RESTORES ALL THINGS.

CHAPTER TWO

The Problem

IN THIS CHAPTER

The Fall
The Hope for this Resource
Hope for Our Brokenness

Although the Fall has affected every area of our lives, God's grace is greater than every sin.

02 / The Problem

The Fall

Although God created sex and sexuality as good gifts, sin distorted God's design. When Adam and Eve disobeyed God in Genesis 3, sin corrupted every corner of the earth. Because of that, our desires are now distorted. Our bodies break down. Brokenness invades all areas of sexuality, gender, and human interactions. Where there was once joy, unity, and love, there is now selfishness, sin, and betrayal. Where there had been freedom and beauty in sexual expression, there is now evidence of hurt, abuse, and shame. Even our bodies show signs of the Fall because of the brokenness the Fall caused. Infertility haunts couples who long for children, and medical conditions affect many, impairing their ability to enjoy sex with their husbands. Our sex and sexuality have both been altered by the Fall.

The curse of sin has affected the entire world. For example, God designed the covenant of marriage to be lifelong, but unfortunately, couples often separate because of the Fall. Death, sin, adultery, and divorce often bring division from the lifelong covenant that God designed for marriage. Similarly, although sex was created for pleasure and blessing, it is often twisted for selfish gain. Children are abused, partners cheat on their spouses, and sexual expression is prioritized over obedience to God.

Not only this, but sexual sins have become viewed as highly-praised rights in western society. It is no longer taboo in most circles to watch pornography or masturbate. Instead of shamefully going to the edge of town to buy a magazine covered in a brown paper bag so that no one will see it, we now have access to unlimited pictures on our phones with the push of a button. Our phones follow us to work, the bedroom, and the bathroom. Temptations like pornography not only surround us but are encouraged as enjoyable "rights" by television, media, friends, and family. Because of modern culture wars for gender and sexuality, the Christian sex ethic is now seen by many as oppressive and hateful.

Our view of sin is too light, and our view of God is too small. We justify and explain our sins away as if we simply forgot to buy something on our list at the grocery store—an inconvenience, to be sure, but not holy treason against a righteous God. And yet, Scripture affirms that our sin against God is so severe that it required the death of God's own Son to forgive us. God is holy, and He will not be mocked. He is perfectly just, and yet, He is also abundantly merciful to provide a way for our salvation. As R. C. Sproul said in his book *The Holiness of God* (121–122):

> The Cross was at once the most horrible and the most beautiful example of God's wrath. It was the most just and the most gracious act in history. God would have been more than unjust, He would have been diabolical to punish Jesus if Jesus had not first willingly taken on Himself the sins of the world. Once Christ had done that, once He volunteered to be the Lamb of God, laden with our sin, then He became the most grotesque and vile thing on the planet. With the concentrated load of sin He carried, He became utterly repugnant to the Father. God poured out His wrath on this obscene thing. God made Christ accursed for the sin He bore. Herein was God's holy justice perfectly manifest. Yet it was done for us. He took what justice demanded for us.

Because of the Fall, we were separated from God in our sins. But thanks be to God—there is hope for every man, woman, and child through Jesus Christ. Jesus paid for our every sinful action, lustful thought, and impure desire on the cross. He not only forgives all who trust in Him, but He also gives us His Spirit, who lives inside of us and transforms us into His image. He clothes us with His righteousness and covers us with His grace. Although the Fall has affected every area of our lives, God's grace is greater than every sin.

Our view of sin is too light, and our view of God is too small.

Romans 1:22–25

Claiming to be wise, they became fools and exchanged the glory of the immortal God for images resembling mortal man, birds, four-footed animals, and reptiles.

Therefore God delivered them over in the desires of their hearts to sexual impurity, so that their bodies were degraded among themselves. They exchanged the truth of God for a lie, and worshiped and served what has been created instead of the Creator, who is praised forever. Amen.

The Hope for This Resource

Sexual sin is pervasive. It affects our thoughts, bodies, and minds. It can make us withdraw from God in shame and lead to division within our relationships. Because of the nature of this booklet, we cannot cover every specific topic of sexual sin or brokenness. Each situation is unique, and the details of sexual sin or brokenness in your life may differ from the situations described. But while each case may vary, the Bible has universal and unchanging hope for the hurting, broken, ashamed, and sinful. It can bring healing to the victim and restoration to the fallen. The gospel of Jesus can redeem and restore every area of sexual sin and brokenness.

Throughout this booklet, be mindful of how each topic is affecting you. If possible, discuss what you've read with a trusted friend and share any concerns, temptations, or fears. This booklet is divided into several main categories: pornography and masturbation, purity in marriage, abuse, homosexuality and transgenderism, and difficult emotions related to sexuality. Within each category, we will seek to address the associated underlying heart issues and share the hope of the gospel for each situation. Finally, we will suggest practical application as you seek to resist temptation and love others well.

As you read, may God protect your heart and your mind. It is our prayer that God exposes any hidden sin or shame and brings hope and healing to the broken crevices of your life. His grace is deep, and His love is sufficient. May our merciful God bring healing and restoration to your sexuality.

> *The Bible has universal and unchanging hope for the hurting, broken, ashamed, and sinful.*

Hope for Our Brokenness

While the effects of sin are devastating, the hope of the gospel is greater. Throughout this booklet, we will strive to continually keep in mind the four truths from page 7. While we might not always address each point verbatim, our overall approach to the complex topics covered in this book will be guided by these four truths:

1. *God is good.*
2. *God's plans are good.*
3. *God forgives and restores.*
4. *The Spirit of God empowers us to live holy lives.*

Because of the gospel, there is hope for our sex and sexuality. God can redeem not only our souls but also our physical bodies through His redemptive work on the cross. There is no sexual sin or shame that God's healing cannot reach. Instead, there is great hope for the one who is addicted to pornography and overwhelmed by the cycle of desire, sin, and shame. There is hope for the one who is tempted to have an affair because of years of marital disappointment. There is hope for every sinner who places his or her trust in Christ because of God's mercy and grace. Through the gospel, God saves us, restores us, redeems us, and makes us new. Although we were once stuck in our sexual sin and brokenness, He has set us free. The Apostle Paul says it this way in 1 Corinthians 6:9–11 (emphasis added):

> Don't you know that the unrighteous will not inherit God's kingdom? Do not be deceived: No sexually immoral people, idolaters, adulterers, or males who have sex with males, no thieves, greedy people, drunkards, verbally abusive people, or swindlers will inherit God's kingdom. *And some of you used to be like this.* But you were washed, you were sanctified, you were justified in the name of the Lord Jesus Christ and by the Spirit of our God.

Although we were once defined by our sin—helpless and hopeless—God has given us a new identity in Christ. There is hope for our sexual sin and brokenness through the perfect Son of God, who washes us, sanctifies us, and justifies us through His Spirit.

THERE IS HOPE FOR OUR SEXUAL
SIN AND BROKENNESS

*through the perfect
Son of God.*

Gospel Hope for Sexual Sin and Brokenness

CHAPTER THREE

Pornography and Masturbation

IN THIS CHAPTER

"Help, I'm Struggling with Pornography."
"Help, My Husband Is Struggling with Pornography."

God can free you from every lustful thought and forgive you for every sin.

03 / Pornography and Masturbation

"Help, I'm Struggling with Pornography."

What is Pornography?

Pornography is defined as "the depiction of erotic behavior (as in pictures or writing) intended to cause sexual excitement" (Merriam-Webster). It is not a problem just for men, nor is it limited to magazine pictures or online videos. Instead, women are regularly drawn into the snares of pornography through the alluring writing of erotic novels, the ease of interactive websites, and the popularization of sensual television shows. These kinds of written and visual pornography can lead to lust, masturbation, fantasy, and erotic thoughts.

If you have watched pornography or struggle with a pornography addiction, you are not alone. Pornography is a growing epidemic among women, and studies show that pornography is not just for men. At the same time, pornography is not in line with God's good design for your sexuality. God created sex to be between a man and a woman in marriage, yet in our minds, we regularly lust through pornographic pictures, videos, erotica, and fantasies. We desire someone who is not our husband, and in the New Testament, Jesus names this lust "adultery" (Matthew 5:27–28). As a consequence, our sin separates us from God (Isaiah 59:2, Romans 3:23).

While pornography can be an ensnaring and devastating addiction, there is hope. God can free you from every lustful thought and forgive you for every sin. Through Christ's hard-won victory on the cross, He made a way for you to be cleansed from the darkness of pornography. He has set you free from its power. And by God's grace, you can be set free from pornography's addictive hold and find healing in your relationships. You can find forgiveness for your sins and hope for tomorrow as God purifies you and changes you to look more like Him. He is faithful, and He will protect and sanctify you. He has made you clean.

Heart Issues

If you view pornography, why do you watch it? Are you tempted to pull up a website or take out a magazine because of lust, dissatisfaction in your marriage, or a desire to escape? As we discuss some possible motivations for your pornography usage over the next several pages, our hope is that this will just be the beginning. Use this section as a primer that prompts you deeper into the Word to uncover what Scripture has to say about lust, idolatry, intimacy, and pleasure.

Dissatisfaction in Marriage and Loneliness

Maybe your pornography addiction was fueled by your desire for a man who listens, protects, or cares for you. Your husband can be insensitive. He's brutish and out of shape, but the man on the pornographic website seems so kind and caring. Though he's not real, he feels more like your soulmate than the man you sleep next to in bed each night. Even in the best marriages, we are all sinners who will disappoint one another. No person was meant to fulfill our every desire because, ultimately, we were made for Christ. But when our needs are not satisfied, Christ doesn't excuse us from looking elsewhere, whether through a computer screen or an attractive coworker. Instead, He encourages us to find contentment in Him. He tells us to consider others as more important than ourselves (Philippians 2:3). In humility, we are to press into God, pray, and ask for help.

God desires you to have a healthy marriage rooted in Him and filled with love, respect, and joy.

If you are feeling dissatisfied in your marriage, identify a few specific areas of tension in your relationship and pray over them. Plan a time to talk to your husband in humility, admitting your own faults and seeking forgiveness for your sin. Consider also seeking counsel as a couple from a trusted third-party, such as your local pastor or a biblical counselor. God desires you to have a healthy marriage rooted in Him and filled with love, respect, and joy. He can restore and redeem even the most difficult of marriages. There is hope because of His mercy and grace.

03: Pornography and Masturbation

Addiction

For many men and women around the world, pornography isn't just a "bad habit." It's a compulsive addiction. Formed over years of daily—if not hourly—indulgences, pornography has become as essential as food. Just like addictive substances, watching pornography releases neurological chemicals like dopamine. This causes the body to feel happy for a moment, but when pornography is viewed often, it can change the neurological makeup of the brain and result in increasingly self-destructive behaviors (Hilton). The problem is that the temporary satisfaction of pornography lasts only for a moment and is quickly followed by a harrowing low. While watching pornography, you feel good as your body releases endorphins that lead you to feel pleasure. But after the endorphins fade, you crave it again. So before long, you find yourself looking at more and more pictures, and what started as a popular erotic fiction book turns into the desire for "just one more" release.

Changing our patterns of addiction requires a holistic and focused effort of our minds, souls, bodies, and hearts. We need the Lord's help, and thankfully, He is powerful enough to free us from sin's heavy grip. We are no longer defined as "beyond help" or "pornography addicts" but as beloved daughters of Christ. If you are struggling with addiction, God has not abandoned you, and in Him, there is great hope for freedom. You are not "too much" for God. He loves you, even in your sin. As you seek God and begin to break cycles of sexual sin, be patient. Addictions formed over years can take time to break. But God is more powerful than anyone or anything, and He has the power to change you and set you free from every bond of addiction.

Note: If you have a history of abuse, your sexual desires may have been awakened from an early age, and pornography and masturbation may have become a soothing pattern for you. At a neurological level, you may view sexual pleasure as a form of relaxation. You may feel a confusing pull to porn, even while being repulsed by it at the same time. Or you may find comfort and safety in the distance pornography creates between a physical person and sexual pleasure. If you have not already, talk to your local pastor and find a trusted biblical counselor to process your history of abuse and find biblical hope and healing.

Lust

Do you view pornography because of your lust? Your body and soul crave physical satisfaction. Your lust consumes you and feels like an unstoppable force. Thankfully, there is hope through the gospel for lust. The answer is found neither from excusing our sin nor from running from it. Rather it is found through repentance and faith in Jesus. If you have trusted in Jesus as your Lord and Savior, He has forgiven you for every sinful thought, attitude, and action. You are no longer under condemnation and shame because He has paid your debt. Now, He clothes you with His righteousness, perfection, and purity. You are made clean, not because you had a perfect week on the internet but because of Jesus. He longs for you to find freedom from this sin and live into the reality of your new identity in Christ.

A Desire for Intimacy

For many women, pornography creates a fantastical connection with another person. Like candy, pornography satisfies our cravings like a cheap and corrosive ruse. It fuels our desires for connection while leaving us empty.

Ultimately, our longing for intimacy is a God-given desire. The God of the universe created us to walk closely with Him, but the intimacy we crave is not found on a computer screen. It is found first and foremost through intimate communion with our Maker (Psalm 139:1–6). God loves you, sees you, and knows you. He listens to your every prayer. He knows what makes you excited and your biggest pet peeve. He knows the stressors in your day and the times that you feel lonely. Even when you feel unsatisfied, unknown, and unloved in other relationships, remember this: God takes care of you as a close, loving Father. Your desire for intimacy will not be satisfied through pornography. You can only be truly fulfilled, satisfied, known, and loved through Christ.

> *You can only be truly fulfilled, satisfied, known, and loved through Christ.*

Escapism

Sometimes, due to the stress of home, work, or daily life, we adopt sinful and destructive habits to help us cope with life's pain. Pornography becomes an unhealthy coping mechanism to release stress and distract ourselves from the overwhelming nature of daily responsibilities. We want to be happy and for problems to disappear. So, we seek temporary peace through sexual sin. But as you've likely experienced firsthand, this kind of rest never truly satisfies. The release of pornography is not followed by rest and peace but by feelings of guilt, shame, and an unquenchable desire for more.

True rest is found not in viewing naked pictures on a computer screen. It is found in Christ (Matthew 11:28–30). When you feel a strong urge to escape life through pornography, remember: Christ is better than pornography. Jesus is better than every temporary pleasure that dulls our senses and feeds our flesh. He is better than the greatest pleasures this world has to offer us. Although we try to escape the troubles of life through pornography, it will never truly satisfy us. True relief, comfort, and hope are found only in Christ. As we bring Him our hurts and our struggles, we find our rest in Him.

> *Jesus is better than every temporary pleasure that dulls our senses and feeds our flesh.*

Masturbation

Porn and masturbation often go together. Whether out of physical lust, a desire to escape, or discontentment in your sex life, you take matters into your own hands and sexually please yourself. Masturbation is "solo sex" that relies on yourself to bring pleasure and satisfaction (Chesnut). Although some therapists promote that masturbation is a healthy way to satisfy your sexual longings, when we look to Scripture, we see that God designed sex to be relational. Therefore, masturbating and sexually satisfying yourself does not follow God's good design.

At times, because of deployment, grief, or sickness, couples may go for a season without having sexual relations. Such circumstances, however, do not give us the right to satisfy ourselves sexually but instead call us to demonstrate self-control. In fact, contrary to popular belief, the need for sexual self-control does not end when we get married. Rather, it looks different throughout life's changing seasons. Abstinence, for a season, can be a way to glorify God and love your spouse.

Some couples wonder if it is okay to masturbate if their husbands approve or if they are thinking about their spouse. But when we look back to God's original design for sex, we see that sex is meant to be between two people in the context of marriage. When we masturbate, we have no need to show patience, kindness, or love to another. We can create a world of our own fantasy, which does not reflect the reality of our lives. Even if we are thinking about our spouses while masturbating, we are not experiencing the covenantal, relational love that God designed for sex.

In Christ alone, we can be fully and deeply satisfied.

Resisting temptation is difficult, and denying the flesh is an active part of the Christian life. Though God may allow us to go through seasons of "longing," He promises to use each trial to refine us in His image (Romans 8:28). Saying "no" to sinful passions makes us look more like Christ—this is not in an attempt to earn God's love but rather in response to it. The Bible reminds us that in Christ alone, we can be fully and deeply satisfied. He equips and sustains us each day through life's struggles. He is enough for us. God controls our future, and He has good plans for us.

As we resist temptation, we remember that though we will have unfulfilled longings in this life, one day, every longing will be fulfilled. We will see Jesus face to face and experience greater pleasure than we could ever imagine. Our momentary longings will be fulfilled, and we will be with our Savior, enjoying Him forever.

Watching Porn Together in Marriage

Some married couples find it arousing to watch pornography together. It feels like pornography is helping their marriages, as they are more engaged and sexually active as a couple than ever. But as Christians, we determine what is right and wrong not based on pragmatism or pleasure but based on God's Word.

In order to have a conversation about pornography within marriage, we must look back to God's original plan for marriage and sexuality. From the beginning of the world, God designed man and woman to complement each other in marriage (Genesis 2:18, 23–24). Marriage was created as a picture of God's covenantal, faithful love for us. Sex is intended to be enjoyed between a husband and wife within the confines of marriage. To include other parties in the bedroom, whether physically or via pornography, is not in line with God's good plan for sexuality.

Throughout Scripture, the commands of God are often linked with His unchanging character. God instructs us to keep the marriage bed pure (Hebrews 13:4), keeping ourselves from adultery and sexual immorality because we trust in the perfect justice of God. Even if no one else sees what goes on in the privacy of your bedroom, God sees and knows. When another party is introduced to the bedroom through pornography, it undermines God's design for sexuality and is detrimental to your marriage. God created marriage to be a picture of His covenantal love for us. His love for us is intimate, committed, covenantal, and faithful. When we watch pornography, it distorts God's good design for marriage.

Not only does pornography go against God's Word, but scientific studies have proven that pornography changes the physiological makeup of our brains (Hilton). Over time, it becomes harder to become sexually aroused without pornography, and it requires longer stimulation to become aroused. Although pornography may feel like a "quick fix" to help bring excitement or rejuvenation into the bedroom, it actually hurts your sex life in the long run.

If you have been watching pornography with your husband, prayerfully go to God's Word together. Talk to your pastor and ask for accountability within your local community. God desires that your sex life be enjoyed with your spouse alone, not through the aid of pornography. So find ways to enjoy one another and be creative within the bedroom that do not involve other people. Married sex does not need to be stale. Have an honest conversation with your spouse about your sexual desires and what is attractive to you, and brainstorm creative ways to engage one another within the bedroom. When we are uncertain about the specifics of "what is allowed" by God, we can look to God's Word and His character to remember that His plans are best. God desires what is best for us, and His design is perfect.

> *God created marriage to be a picture of His covenantal love for us. His love for us is intimate, committed, covenantal, and faithful.*

Gospel Hope

So far in this section, we have defined the problem of pornography and masturbation, and we have discussed some of the underlying heart issues surrounding it. Within each section, we have aimed to bring gospel hope and biblical clarity. But now, we will explicitly address the question, "What hope does the gospel bring to us in our struggle against sexual sin?"

Gospel Hope for Sin and Shame

You want to hide. You're embarrassed to the core. Surely other women don't struggle with this kind of sin. Many people call pornography a "guy problem," yet you struggle with it too. To make things worse, you've been keeping secrets and hiding this from your husband. You feel dirty and ashamed.

There is a difference between guilt and shame. Whereas guilt says, "I've done something wrong," shame says, "I *am* wrong; there is something wrong with *me*" (Ed Welch, *Shame Interrupted*). You feel like a disappointment to God and others. *If they knew the extent of my dirtiness, they would never love me*, you think. Shame consumes you and makes you want to hide.

Our shame in watching pornography is further complicated by our sexual backgrounds and upbringings. If you came from a conservative Christian home, for example, you might have been raised to ignore sexual temptations. You might have attended purity conferences and worn "True Love Waits" rings. But that didn't shield you from the brokenness of sexuality. Whether in the forms of lust, pornography, or fantasy, sin invaded your heart, but you felt unable to talk to your friends or family because sex was taboo to discuss. So instead, you sunk into the pit of sin or shame, wondering what was wrong with you. Your purity was your identity, the proof that you were worthy of love. Now that you watch porn, you conclude that you must be worthless.

Or maybe you grew up without any regard for sexual limitations until Christ found you and saved you. But years of trauma, addictions, and scars have become the bony hands that yank you into pits of despair and shame. You think, *The "good Christian girls" in my church would never understand.*

The problem of sin goes back to the beginning of the Bible. In the garden of Eden, when Adam and Eve sinned against God, they felt embarrassed and ashamed. They hid in their nakedness, but God sought them, fully aware of their sin. He covered their nakedness and clothed them. In the same way, when we trust in Jesus, He covers and clothes us with His perfect sacrifice. On the cross, Christ paid our sin debt and bore our shame. We are given God's righteous clothes and made clean by His grace (Zechariah 3:3–5).

In Christ, there is hope not only for our guilt but also for our shame. Even when our inward selves condemn us, we can be confident that God no longer does (Romans 8:1). When we want to hide, we can know that God pursues us and covers us with His perfect covering (Genesis 3:9–11, 21). He has given us a new identity—a gospel identity—that is founded on His unchanging character. We are loved, accepted, and known. We are beloved, forgiven, and free through Jesus.

Not only this, but God is not embarrassed by or squeamish about our sexuality. As created by God, sex is not shameful, nor is it dirty. It is a good gift given by God to be enjoyed within certain boundaries. We can go to God with our sexual struggles, knowing that God created sex and is not embarrassed by our bodies. He designed us as sexual beings, and He has covered our sexual sins through the cross.

God cares for you. He has mercy on you. When He sees you stuck in sin, like an animal trapped in a net, He desires to set you free from what is hurting you. As one who was tempted in every way but was without sin, Christ has compassion on you (Hebrews 4:15). He loves you, even in your sin and shame, and He has set you free from the power of shame because of the cross.

We are loved, accepted, and known. We are beloved, forgiven, and free through Jesus.

Forgiveness in Christ

After viewing pornography, you may wonder, *Have I sinned too much? How could God forgive me when I've struggled with this sin for so long?* Yet the scandal of the gospel is that through the perfect life, death, and resurrection of Jesus, those who trust in Him are forgiven of all their sins. This includes every sin of sexual fantasy and lust. God didn't wait until we were clean enough or until we were deserving of His love to save us. He didn't wait until we hadn't viewed pornography for three weeks or thirty years. Rather, He saved us while we were His enemies (Romans 5:10).

He saved us, knowing the full extent and depravity of our sins yet still showing incomprehensible mercy on us. On the cross, Jesus paid the penalty for every moment you viewed pornography and for your every lustful thought. As He breathed His last breath, He uttered, "It is finished" (John 19:30). The payment for sins is complete for all who would trust in Jesus. This includes the sins of viewing pornography, as well as every sin that so often surrounds it (including the sins of lying, deceit, neglecting God-given responsibilities, sins of omission, etc.). As Christians, we can approach the throne of God with confidence, knowing we have been forgiven for every sin. This is not because of our own goodness but because of the perfection of Christ.

Spirit-Empowered Self-Control

If you are a Christian, there is lasting hope for you because of Christ. When you repented of your sin and placed your trust in Jesus, God not only promised to forgive you of every sin but also gave you His Holy Spirit to live inside of you. The Spirit convicts us of sin (John 16:8), gives wisdom (Ephesians 1:17), and empowers us to live godly lives (Ephesians 3:14–19). The Bible then concludes that if we have been raised with Christ, we are to live by the Spirit (Galatians 5:16, 25) and put to death the deeds of the flesh, including sexual sin (Colossians 3:1–11).

As we now move into a section offering practical steps to take in your struggle against pornography, remember: God loves you. There is hope for change. As a Christian, you have the Spirit living inside you to equip you for self-control. He forgives us of our sins. He loves us, and He can change you.

Practical Help

Pray

Prayer reminds us that we can do nothing without God's help. God is not only the author of our salvation, but He is also the source of our sanctification—our growing in Christlikeness. He wants us to trust Him with every struggle and ask Him for help in every battle. Spend time now praying to the Lord. If you are unsure what to pray, open the Bible to Psalm 51, and read the words of Scripture back to God. Ask for His help to break free from your bondage to pornography. God wants you to trust Him and to be free from this sin, and He knows that you cannot do it on your own. Ask the Lord for help in your fight against sexual temptation.

Tell Your Husband

Sin loves the dark. When it's hidden, it grows and morphs like bacteria festering in a moist test tube. Because of your guilt and shame, you may be tempted to want to hide your sin from your husband. You've sinned against him, and you don't know how he will react. You feel ashamed in light of how deeply he has loved you. You don't want to hurt him. However, even though it can be difficult to confess sin, biblical counselor Ed Welch reminds us in an article titled *Disclose or Be Exposed* that "confession is more important than consequences." After we sin, we honor God by confessing our sins and turning from them, regardless of the consequences.

As you share your sexual sin with your husband, be mindful that he could respond in different ways. Give him space to process the sin, and understand that healing can take time. Invite him to help you create a plan against pornography. If your husband has a history of outbursts of anger or if you feel scared to talk with him, meet with your pastor or a biblical counselor first to discuss practical ways to create a safe space for honest confessions.

Find Accountability Partners

Pornography isolates. Through it, the enemy wants to keep you hidden in the dark, stuck in your sin and shame. Part of breaking pornography's grip on your soul is to bring sin into the light and build a biblical community around you. Be a part of a godly local church. Sit under the teaching of the Word of God each week. Be involved in a Bible study, and find a local ministry that addresses sexual sin. Create a team of trusted friends who know about your sin and who will help hold you accountable.

Internet Controls

John Owen once wrote, "Be killing sin, or sin will be killing you." If we want to be serious about killing our addiction to pornography, we must take action and create a plan to remove temptations for sin. If your television, phone, or computer are tools that aid your pornography usage, create healthy boundaries to remove this temptation.

Websites such as Covenant Eyes also provide healthy internet boundaries to pornography websites and allow you to give access to your browsing history to your spouse or a trusted friend. Delete any images from your phone, delete the backup trash bin, and set up controls with your internet service provider. Make a preemptive plan to restrict your phone or computer usage, and share it with a trusted friend. Include your husband as you make a plan, and ask what restrictions he would like to create to reestablish trust.

Evaluate Triggers

Take an honest inventory of your sin by intentionally dissecting your moments of temptation. Evaluate your triggers to sin, and consider questions such as, When do I sin? Where do I sin? Are there any patterns in my spiritual, personal, or emotional life that make me more susceptible to sin? Consider your habits of sin so that you can set up appropriate internet controls. When, where, and how are you most likely to view pornography? If you discover that you mainly view pornography on your phone after a long day at work, for example, set phone restrictions after work. Don't take your phone into the bathroom or bedroom with you at the end of the day. Use an old-fashioned alarm clock to wake you up, and leave your phone in the kitchen. Or better still, get a "dumb phone" for emergency calls, and leave your smartphone at work or with a friend at the end of the day.

After You Sin

You feel ashamed. You have been trying so hard. You even found victory over your sin—until yesterday. *How could you mess up again? Haven't you learned?* You condemn yourself with the anger of one who has walked this road many times before. Whereas modern psychology might encourage you to ignore your feelings of sexual guilt, God offers more. He desires for you to find restoration, healing, and forgiveness in Him. We have a compassionate High Priest in Jesus, even when we fail (Hebrews 4:15). Jesus knows what it feels like to experience excruciating temptation (Matthew 4:1–11). He was tempted in every way, yet He stood firm in His fight against sin. We can pray to Him as One who understands our struggles and sympathizes with our weaknesses yet perfectly fulfilled the Father's will. Not only this, but because of Jesus's resurrection, we can have hope. Jesus has defeated the power and penalty of sin in our lives. We are no longer defined by our sins, condemned, and alone in the world. We are given a new identity as forgiven heirs of the King because of the gospel. As a result, we can grieve our sins with faith and grow in awe of His holiness and grace. Jesus delights in showing mercy to sinners like us.

> *God offers more. He desires for you to find restoration, healing, and forgiveness in Him.*

So, after you sin, run to the Lord. Ask for His forgiveness again, knowing that His mercy is great. Confess your sin to your husband and accountability partner, and retroactively evaluate your triggers to better understand your moment of weakness. What were the temptations that led up to your sin? How was pornography accessible to you, and how can you limit access for future temptations? What were you thinking, feeling, and wanting—before, during, and after? Learn to take your thoughts captive by regular time in the Word (2 Corinthians 10:5). Take responsibility for your actions, and turn back to the Lord.

When you sin, make it your aim to turn to the Lord and repent faster each time. Also, spend time recognizing the ways you've grown in your struggle against temptation. Maybe in the past, you regularly viewed porn or masturbated multiple times a day. Now, it's been two weeks since you fell into that sin. Although the return to sin can be discouraging, it is also important to recognize that God has been growing you. There is hope for change.

Although you may fail, the Lord's grace is greater than your sin. So don't give up. As you fight against sin, pursue progress, not perfection. Don't get derailed if you're not sinless right away. Rather, continue to strive for holiness. Our goal is to grow in Christlikeness, not to become instantly perfect. When you fail, run to Jesus, your greatest friend and Savior.

The Expulsive Power of a New Affection

Many women want an easy fix in their fight against pornography. They want to be able to "just stop it." To do better. To be better. They create boundaries and accountability, and they do better for a season, only to fall into deeper sin. Or, for some, they gain victory over one sin just to replace it with another. They no longer watch pornography as regularly but instead overindulge in drugs, alcohol, or other destructive behaviors. But in order to break free from our love of pornography, we must have an even greater love. Scottish minister Thomas Chalmers calls this the "expulsive power of a new affection."

As you create plans and take honest, God-glorifying steps toward fighting sin, remember Christ. Look to Him. Be satisfied in Him. Fall in love with Him. Your battle against sin will be won through a greater, more satisfying love found only in Christ. One day, the battle will end, and you will see Christ face to face as you enjoy Him forever. Your faith will be made sight, and every sacrifice of obedience will be rewarded. He will reveal His victory over sin once and for all, and we will be healed.

> *"Your battle against sin will be won through a greater, more satisfying love found only in Christ."*

Battling Pornography Checklist

- [ ] Confess your sin to the Lord. Be specific, confessing not only your sin of pornography but also the lusts of your heart, deception, etc.
- [ ] Make a plan to tell your husband.
- [ ] Tell your husband.
- [ ] Confess to a trusted female friend.
- [ ] Evaluate your triggers and patterns of pornography.
- [ ] Identify your idols and the corresponding gospel hope.
- [ ] Create appropriate boundaries against pornography, considering your:
  - Access to credit cards
  - Internet access, usage, and passwords
  - Internet or television controls
- [ ] Create an accountability team. Plan a regular time to connect.
- [ ] Get biblical counseling.
- [ ] Write down verses that will help you in the midst of temptation.
- [ ] Make a list of why you do not want to sin, and place it in a place you will see it.
- [ ] Remember your gospel identity.
- [ ] Find hope in the cross and the resurrection of Jesus over all sin.
- [ ] Pray.

"Help, My Husband Is Struggling with Pornography."

The Problem

If you are reading this section, you have likely had the gut-dropping experience of finding pornography on your husband's phone or computer. Studies suggest that between 50–90% of husbands have viewed pornography (Madison). Studies also show that the feelings a wife experiences after discovering her husband's pornography typically mirror the emotions of adultery victims (Simonyi-Gindele). Thus, if you are among the majority of this statistic, you've likely experienced a wide range of emotions. In shock, you've likely vacillated between shame, fury, and insecurity. In fear and anger, you've wondered, *How could he?* Yet you've simultaneously felt terrified to see how deep the pit of destruction goes. You may have asked questions like, *Is there something wrong with me? Am I not enough? What did I do wrong?*

It is important to state from the beginning of this section that your husband's sin is not your fault. Each one of us is responsible before the Lord for our own sins, and your husband is responsible before the Lord for his sins of pornography, lust, and deception. His sin is, first and foremost, against a holy God, and it is egregious to Him. God does not minimize or discount your husband's sin just because he is a male who has urges.

There is hope for your husband and your marriage.

In most cases, the problem of pornography existed long before marriage. Your husband has likely struggled for years with problems such as lust, idolatry, escapism, or desire for pleasure. But instead of seeking fulfillment through Christ and within your marriage, he sought cheap, addictive substitutes. Scripture calls men, young and old, to be self-controlled (Titus 2:2, 6), but by viewing pornography, your husband not only disregarded commands within Scripture, but he also dishonored you. Even so, through Christ, there is also great hope for forgiveness and healing. God can forgive and redeem even the worst of sinners. He can break the bonds of addiction and restore marriages. There is hope for your husband and your marriage.

In the following few pages, we will be discussing how to confront your husband about his sin and how to find personal healing. But regardless of the outcome of your husband's progress in recovery, there is hope for you. Through the ups and downs of betrayal, *you are never alone*. God goes before you, and He walks with you. He will never abandon you. There are many, many women who have also experienced the pain of betrayal but who have found the Lord to be a faithful companion through their sorrow. There is joy, peace, healing, and hope available for you in Christ. God will walk with you every step of this journey, and He can bring healing and restoration to your heavy heart. He will never abandon you, and He is your present help in times of need (Psalm 46:1). There is hope for you in Christ.

Heart Issues

Shock. Betrayal. Anger. Fear. Embarrassment. Shame. Horror. After discovering your husband has been watching pornography, you've likely experienced the full spectrum of these emotions. Maybe you've experienced each of these emotions within a single day, hour by hour discovering new depths to your anguish, anger, and fear. The nightmare feels unbearable, and you wonder, *Will this pain ever end?* However, the truth is that this pain will not last forever. So let's take a deep dive into some of these natural emotional responses and the heart issues they can lead us to if we don't process these emotions well. And then we will look at the gospel hope and practical help.

Shock

Perhaps your first emotion after the discovery was shock. When we experience betrayal, grief, or loss, God often allows us to experience a short season of shock in order to adjust to our new reality. Although this is a normal human experience, it will fade in time. When it does, it can be tempting to want to continue in your feelings of numbness by moving into denial, seeking to avoid the pain caused by your husband's sin. Grieving truthfully is an important part of the healing process. True healing comes as we honestly acknowledge our pain and bring it before the Lord. God can handle your raw emotions, and He can bring clarity out of confusion. He is with you as you process the news of your husband's sin. God is not surprised by our emotions, and He provides hope and healing in the midst of betrayal.

Betrayal

Maybe you have experienced deep feelings of betrayal. Your husband broke your trust and has been living two lives. In one sense, it may feel like you're living with a stranger. The man you fell in love with is gone, replaced by an intruder who has hurt you to the core. In another sense, perhaps the distance, irritability, and lack of intimacy within your marriage may seem to make sense now.

Scripture is not quiet on the topic of betrayal. Throughout history, men and women of the Bible have been betrayed, deceived, and dishonored. As we read their stories, we remember that God doesn't condemn you when you are betrayed. He is with you, interceding for you and loving you. He will never betray or abandon you. He will never leave you. He is your shelter, rock, and refuge (Psalm 91:1–2).

Anger, Anxiety, or Shame

Maybe you have also experienced deep feelings of anger, anxiety, or shame. Throughout Scripture, God provides hope and understanding for each of our emotions. God made our emotions, and we can go to Him with every angry thought and fearful doubt. God understands your pain, and He is with you each moment.

Ultimately, there is still hope for your marriage. As dark as this season may feel, there is hope for you and your husband in Christ. There is great hope for his restoration, especially if your husband is honest with his problems and wants to change. Without question, trust has been broken and will take time to rebuild. Your husband is likely feeling great shame, hopelessness, and depression as well (Dickson). He will have a long road of repentance ahead, but do not give up hope for God to repair your marriage and relationship. Through it all, God is with you, and He can redeem even the most desperate of situations.

Gospel Hope for Your Husband's Struggle with Pornography

You Are Not Alone. Christ Also Desires Holiness and Purity in Your Marriage.

For women who feel abandoned during this season, it is important to remember that God is with you. He sees all, and He is the just judge. He cares about the purity of your marriage, and He hates sin. He does not turn a blind eye to your husband's pornography. Rather, God designed marriages to be a reflection of His covenant love and is grieved by your husband's sin. God agrees with you in the wrongdoing of your husband's sin and wants your husband to turn from his rebellion and find life in Him. You do not need to fear, even when you walk through the valley of death, because God is with you (Psalm 23:4). He promises to redeem even the ugliest of life's moments and use them for His glory and our good. He will continue to work in and through your life, even in the midst of pain, shame, or betrayal.

Your Identity Is Secure in the Lord.

You do not need to compete with a photoshopped image. You don't need to get plastic surgery, buy fancy lingerie, or get lip fillers to earn your husband's affection. Your identity is secure in the Lord. God has made you in His image, and you are precious in His sight. Because of the Fall, we live with broken sinners, and your husband is entrapped in sin. As a wife, you may be able to help your husband in his restoration, but his sin is not your sin.

> *Your worth and value are based on the steadfast love of God.*

What's more, your husband's pornography problem is not your fault. Interestingly, a 2012 study showed that a spouse's use of porn was not linked to whether they were sexually satisfied in their marriage (Simonyi-Gindele). Although it can be tempting to blame yourself for your husband's sexual sin, *he* is responsible for his actions. Through it all, you can rest in the knowledge that your worth and value are not based on your husband's faithfulness; your worth and value are based on the steadfast love of God.

Forgiveness and Change Are Possible.

Trust is built over time, and restoration will be a long journey ahead. But through Christ, there is always hope for change and forgiveness. When we forgive someone, we are not saying that what they did is okay. We're not excusing any behavior or saying that it didn't hurt. We may still need to establish healthy boundaries.

Instead, forgiveness is saying that we will not dwell on or bring up their sin to use it against them (Sande). Instead of dwelling on the sins committed against you, you can find rest in the truth that God knows all. He is for you, and He never leaves you. He is the just judge (2 Thessalonians 1:6–12). He can change anyone, and He can do anything. Not only can God change your husband, but He can also supply everything you need to do His will. He can help you grow in joy despite this suffering, and He will make you look more like Christ even through this trial.

Even if Your Marriage Isn't Restored, You Can Be Okay.

God is enough for you. While there is always hope that God can restore your marriage, marriage is not your ultimate hope. If you base your happiness on another person or relationship, you will be disappointed. When you make someone else your source of happiness, you give them the power to control your emotions. When the relationship is going well, you're at the top of the world. When the relationship is struggling, you're driven to the pits of despair. You're like a yoyo with your spouse holding the string. But when we place our hope in the One who never changes, we can find fullness of life and unfaltering joy.

> *Through Christ, there is always hope for change and forgiveness.*

Christ Is the Perfect Bridegroom.

Marriage was designed as a momentary picture of God's love for you, but in heaven, there will be no marriage (Matthew 22:30). In heaven, we'll finally experience the fullness of God's love. We will no longer need the imagery of His love because we will experience its fullness firsthand. We will see Him face to face and experience the sufficiency of His goodness once and for all. Even as we await this day, we remember that God takes care of us. He has given us everything we need (Psalm 23:1). We do not need a good marriage to be fulfilled and happy. We do not need the unfaltering attention of our husbands. We need Christ, and in Him, we have all that we need. His care for us is steadfast and unchangeable. His love lasts forever.

Practical Help

God cares for you. He cares for you in your heartbreak and in your insecurity. He cares for you when you go numb with anger and when the world goes blurry after a panic attack. He listens to your prayers, and He will help you. It is easy for women to feel alone after finding out that their husband has been viewing porn. But although you may feel abandoned, you are never truly alone. The One who made you and loves you will never abandon you. He is with you, holding you, helping you, guiding you, and loving you. He will never betray or leave you.

Pray

As you process the news of your husband's pornography, talk to the Lord and tell Him what you're feeling. Tell Him your complaints, laments, and fears. Pour out your heart to the Lord in moments of sorrow and in moments of fear. Pray for help, healing, and hope. If you have kids, pray for your children. Pray for friends and for biblical community to support you during this season. Pray for the faith to trust God when life hurts, and ask for help forgiving your husband for the ways he has sinned against you.

If you find it difficult to focus while praying, try journaling your prayers or saying them aloud. Read the psalms back to God, and lament the pain and hurt you've experienced. Pray also for your husband. God can do anything, and He can change your husband, as impossible as it may seem. God can break the chains of addiction and restore broken marriages. Advocate for your husband before the throne of grace, and pour out your heart before Him.

Talk to Your Husband

When you find out that your husband has been viewing pornography, you are likely experiencing a roller coaster of emotions. You are grieving the loss of trust and the betrayal of your husband while needing to have an important conversation with him to understand the depths of his sin. This may be one of the most difficult conversations you will experience, so spend time with the Lord before you approach your husband. Ask the Lord for wisdom, and seek His Word for clarity.

In this conversation, you will have the opportunity to honestly respond to your husband in a way that honors God. Although you should aim to speak in a way that is helpful and timely, your husband's repentance is not up to you. You do not need to have the perfect words or approach. God's work does not depend on the eloquence of your speech but on His perfect power. So as you prepare, do not be afraid. You are not alone. God goes before you, and He will defend you.

Tell a Trusted Friend

As a wife, you don't want to embarrass your husband or make him look bad. You've seen the cycle of shame that often accompanies pornography, and you don't want to hurt your husband. At the same time, it is important for you to have a support system as you process your own healing and recovery.

Identify one or two safe friends with whom you can share everything. Tell your husband that you will not spread rumors about him or tell everyone about his pornography usage but that you would like at least one friend to help give you support and godly counsel. Find a friend who will not gossip about you or your husband but who will pray for you and encourage you on the hard days. This friend should support you and your marriage, not encourage needless bashing or complaining about your husband. Rather, she should be a safe person to process your hurt and grief.

When Your Husband Doesn't Listen, Get Help

In an ideal world, after you discover your husband's pornography, you'd see immediate change. You'd be able to go to your husband, and he'd feel remorse. He'd want to change. He'd be grieved that he had hurt you. But at times, the snares of addiction can keep people from seeing clearly. Statistics show that after an initial conversation confronting a husband about his pornography, about 55% of men get help (Dickson). But if your husband is among the remaining 45%, you may need to take additional steps as well.

If your husband does not respond to your approach and continues in a pattern of unrepentant sin, you may need to continue the pattern of confrontation found in Matthew 18:15–20. In these verses, Jesus provides instructions for how believers can approach a fellow Christ-follower who has sinned against them. This process starts first with a one-on-one conversation; then, if that is not successful, it progresses to involving one or two others and then, finally, the church.

Following this model, if your husband does not respond to your one-on-one conversation with him, involve one to two trusted third-party friends. If, after a season, your husband still does not respond, gather a team who can support you and your husband with the help of your pastor. As you move through the confrontation steps of Matthew 18:15–20, continue praying for your husband, remembering that only God can convict and soften hearts. Statistically, 99% of men will respond by getting help after having an intervention, as mentioned in the above steps (Dickson). Continue to pray to the Lord and ask Him to help your husband find freedom from pornography.

Counseling

Biblical counseling can be a helpful tool for many couples. During difficult conversations, a neutral third party—such as your local pastor or a trusted biblical counselor—can help provide biblical wisdom, insight, and help. They can help strengthen communication skills, develop accountability action plans, and establish healthy boundaries.

If your husband is willing, consider seeing a counselor together. Even if he is unwilling, consider seeing the counselor by yourself in order to help you process your feelings of grief, anger, fear, and betrayal. You can find a list of local biblical counselors through websites such as https://biblicalcounseling.com/find-a-counselor/.

Accountability and Local Accountability Ministries

Your husband needs to be sharing the details of his pornography usage with someone. As the offended party, it will likely be difficult for you to remain neutral and dispassionate as his only accountability partner. Therefore, it would be helpful for him to have a trusted male friend to share the intimate details of his sin.

While you cannot force your husband to get help, as his wife, you can encourage him to seek accountability. Ask your husband to discuss the specifics of his sin with a friend, including what he's watched, where, how, and why. If he does not know who to confide in, he can ask your local pastor for recommendations. There may be local Christian accountability ministries and sexual addiction programs to aid in this process as well.

Prayerfully decide how many details you'd like to know about your husband's sin. While some women want to know every detail, others find it more difficult to move forward when they know the specifics. You have the right to ask your husband for information, and you should know the biggest details of his sin (who, what, when, where, why), but be wise about how your mind works and how you respond to excess information. Try not to ask questions out of morbid curiosity but rather so that you can understand the depths of your husband's sin and his need for change.

Healthy Boundaries

In order to rebuild trust, you will need to establish boundaries for the future. Healthy boundaries are designed to help couples grow closer together in the long run. They are not excuses for vengefully hurting your husband, cutting him out of your life because he is difficult, or building emotional walls out of anger. Rather, healthy boundaries are formed for your protection and the good of your marriage. These boundaries should be specific, clear, and carefully established. Make a plan for healthy boundaries, which may include an internet tracking program on your husband's phone and computer, transitioning from a smartphone to a flip phone for a season, and regular check-ins with you and a counselor.

Pursue Forgiveness

Forgiving your husband does not mean that his sin doesn't matter or that he didn't hurt you. It does not mean that his pornography is "not a big deal" or that he doesn't need to change. Rather, it means releasing him of the debt he owes against you. It means not holding it against him with anger and bitterness. It means showing grace, hoping for the best (1 Corinthians 13:7), and enduring with him patiently. It is possible to offer complete forgiveness while not yet trusting someone. Trust is earned through trustworthy behavior over a proven track record. When you forgive your husband, it does not mean that you need to erase any healthy boundaries you've established. But rather, because God has forgiven you, you can forgive your husband for watching pornography (Matthew 18:21–35).

> **"**
>
> *When you forgive your husband, it does not mean that you need to erase any healthy boundaries you've established.*
>
> *But rather, because God has forgiven you, you can forgive your husband for watching pornography.*

CHAPTER FOUR

Purity in Marriage

IN THIS CHAPTER

"Help, I'm Attracted to Someone Who Isn't My Spouse."
"Help, I Don't Want to Have Sex with My Spouse."
"Help, I Have a Greater Sex Drive than My Husband."

We are called to pursue holiness, not only with our actions but also with our minds.

04: Purity in Marriage

04 / Purity in Marriage

"Help, I'm Attracted to Someone Who Isn't My Spouse."

The Problem

It all started with a glance. Though you're married, you've started developing attraction for someone who isn't your spouse. You get dressed in the morning, wondering what he will think about your outfit. You find yourself thinking, *What is he like outside of the gym? I bet he would be a thoughtful husband or great in the bedroom.* Or maybe, your attraction to someone who isn't your spouse started innocently enough with your "work husband." You gave your coworker this pet name because you get along so well at work. You share inside jokes, snacks, and office secrets. Now, after a rough spot in your marriage, you've started to develop real, romantic feelings toward your coworker.

For many women, attraction may also develop for someone they have never met in person. Reality dating shows capture the affection and attraction of thousands of women. As they buy into an often curated, insincere television persona, they become dissatisfied with the real men who are in front of them. *Surely,* they think, *the star of this show would never have morning breath or bad hair days. Surely, this man would listen, be kind, and take care of his body. I just know he would change a baby's diaper at 3:00 a.m. because he is perfect, thoughtful, and kind.* Our futures seem to become brighter and more cheerful in the arms of an imaginary man.

While it is normal to become attracted to another person at some point in marriage, as Christians, we are held to a higher standard. We are called to pursue holiness, not only with our actions but also with our minds. Jesus said that whenever we lust after another man, we commit adultery in our hearts (Matthew 5:27–28). We are to keep the marriage bed pure (Hebrews 13:4), which involves more than not sleeping with another person. It also refers to the thoughts and passions of our hearts. Scripture calls us to be devoted to our spouses alone (Proverbs 5:18, Ephesians 5:22–23, 1 Peter 3:1–2).

But what if you are already ensnared in lust or attraction for a person who is not your spouse? The following pages will help evaluate the heart motives for this attraction, as well as establish clear boundaries to guard your marriage.

Heart Issues

What is at the heart of your attraction? Are you discontent in your marriage or unsatisfied with the husband God has given you? Have there been painful moments in your marriage that have led to disconnectedness and division? Do you imagine that life with someone else would be better—easier, healthier, funnier, or happier? Or has your husband let himself go physically, and over time, you've grown attracted to someone else's body, consumed by the flame of lust?

Very regularly, our growing attraction for another person is rooted in our own discontentment. We are not happy, and we assume that someone else could satisfy the deep longings of our bodies or souls. Yet the Bible tells us that our happiness is not found in the perfect spouse, job, or house. Our contentment is rooted in Christ. This means that we can remain content and faithful to God's commands regardless of the worthiness or attractiveness of our respective spouses.

It is possible to notice that someone else is attractive without lusting over them. Whenever someone attractive catches our eye, we can be aware of their attractiveness while redirecting our gaze and reaffirming our affection for our spouse alone. Through discipline and covenantal commitment, we can develop eyes for our spouses alone. The problem is that often, we feed and fuel our temptations. What may begin as an impulse of physical attraction is nurtured like a small seed. We water our affections with frequent attention and fertilize them with our vivid imaginations. We let our thoughts of another linger in our minds and grow.

Through the gospel, redemption and reconciliation are always possible.

Yet through the gospel, we can be content in all circumstances, even with a sinful spouse. The reality is that every married woman is married to a sinful man, and in the course of your marriage, your husband will disappoint you, fail you, and sin against you. Even so, through the gospel, redemption and reconciliation are always possible. Even if your husband fails you, gains one hundred pounds, or doesn't lead you well, you can stay firmly rooted in the promises of God. You can resist the temptation to idolize or lust after someone else. Scripture calls us to think about what is true, helpful, and good (Philippians 4:8). Instead of meditating on and fueling attraction toward someone who is not your spouse, you are to turn to the Lord and be satisfied with the groom of your youth (Proverbs 5:18).

The secret to a happy life is not based on our circumstances, including the worthiness of our husbands. It is rooted in Christ. As Christians, we may still experience feelings of unhappiness in our marriages. We may still have pain, conflict, and disappointment. Even so, we can have joy because of the hope that Christ offers. We can be content and resist temptation, even with an imperfect husband, because Christ is perfect, and He is enough for us.

Gospel Hope

Through the gospel, Jesus has made a way for our sins to be forgiven. When we believe in Christ's finished work on the cross, God's forgiveness reaches past our abstract sins to our particular sins. His grace touches our most personal, embarrassing, and sensitive offenses. He forgives us when we lust over a coworker or idolize a television celebrity. He cleanses us of any sexual advances we've made toward someone who isn't our spouse. The blood of Jesus forgives us of every sin. If you have sinned against your spouse through your thoughts or actions toward another person, there is forgiveness for you at the foot of the cross. You can humbly go to your spouse, ask for their forgiveness, and make amends, as appropriate, because you have been forgiven by your Maker.

> **"**
>
> *There is always hope for us in Christ.*

At the same time, the love of Christ does not leave us stuck in our sin. Our sin brings division and hurt to our marriages, but God desires greater fulfillment for our lives. God doesn't want us to stay burdened by secret sins or adulterous hearts; God wants us to have marriages that are full of love, acceptance, honesty, joy, and freedom. So as we grow in grace, we are to actively turn away from sexual sin and pursue righteousness. In response to God's all-sufficient love, we can commit to a future of purity and reverence, knowing that God's Spirit is at work within us, helping us to resist temptation for His glory. There is always hope for us in Christ. As we repent before God and to our husbands, we can find freedom, joy, and a very present help in our times of need.

Practical Help

Create Healthy Boundaries with the Opposite Sex.

Many godly men and women have fallen into sin without preemptively scheming to destroy their marriages. What started as innocent affection for another person slowly developed into lust and eventually gave way to sexual sin. Boundaries were unhelpful or ignored, and secrets reigned.

Because sin loves to hide, make plans for regular, honest conversations with your spouse about the opposite sex. Talk about his comfort level with your current relationships, and share your comfort level with him as well. Discuss healthy boundaries, especially given your previous history of attraction toward someone else. While there is biblical freedom regarding the specifics of these boundaries, use wisdom and recognize that we are all vulnerable to temptation.

As Christians, we should live in a way that is above reproach to a watching world. Because we have been saved by grace, our lives should look different than those around us. For example, out of a desire to honor their wives, many pastors will never be alone in a closed room with a member of the opposite sex. As they practically live above reproach, they also affirm the truth that adultery can never happen if there is no opportunity for it to happen.

The Bible also tells us to make no provision for the flesh (Romans 13:14). This means that we should not only avoid sexual sin but also avoid putting ourselves in compromising situations. Maybe in your workplace, you must regularly have one-on-one meetings or take work trips with a member of the opposite sex. Even so, consider ways that you can honor your spouse in the workplace. Maybe you can keep the door open during one-on-one meetings. Maybe you can travel at a different time than your coworker, eat meals on your own rather than sharing them with your coworker, and have regular check-ins with your spouse. Especially if you have developed attraction toward your coworker, create strong boundaries to protect your marriage, and keep no secrets from your spouse.

Don't take chances with your marriage by putting yourself in compromising situations. Instead, create a healthy, transparent relationship with your spouse, full of love and trust.

Pursue Self-Control and Accountability.

The Scriptures are full of admonitions for self-control. For example, Proverbs 25:28 says that a man without self-control is like a city without walls. In other words, in the same way that an Old Testament city without walls was vulnerable to the attacks of neighboring enemies, we are vulnerable to the schemes of sin if we do not have self-control.

We are vulnerable to the schemes of sin if we do not have self-control.

In the New Testament, the apostles also wrote about the importance of self-control (Titus 2:5, 2 Peter 1:5–7). They explained that we are to put off and put on certain behaviors—including certain sexual thoughts, desires, and actions—and put on the righteousness of Christ. We are to put off any form of sexual sin, including lust, and have eyes for our spouse alone. This is an active process of growing in self-discipline and worship of the Lord. With the Spirit's help, we can grow in self-control with regard to our sexual thoughts and actions.

As Christians, we must practice restraint and self-control with our thoughts, retraining and restraining them from sin. As previously stated, there is a difference between noticing that someone is attractive and letting your thoughts linger on them. When you notice your mind start wandering toward someone of the opposite sex, recognize what is happening and tell a female friend who can help keep you accountable.

Repent of any sinful lusts and redeem your mind by thinking about things that honor the Lord. Not only this, but also prepare for moments of temptation before they come. Write a "temptation action plan" by compiling a list of what you will think about or do in moments of temptation. Use the template below to begin this preparation.

"When I am tempted I will..." (List actions such as *tell my spouse*, *tell my accountability partner*, *go for a run*, *get outside*, or *recite the following verses*):

_____

_____

_____

_____

_____

"When I am tempted to lust after someone who is not my spouse, I will think about..." List helpful Bible verses and thoughts below.

_____

_____

_____

_____

Tell Your Spouse and Consider Counseling.

Tell your husband about your attraction. Sin loves the dark, and hiding sin from your spouse may be tempting because you know confessing your sin will hurt him. But by hiding your sin, you compound the sin of lusting after another person by lying and keeping secrets from your spouse. Communication is essential for a healthy marriage, and talking with your husband about your thoughts, temptations, and sins is important.

As you confess your attraction to another person to your husband, plan your words and pick a good time without the distraction of kids or commitments. Come with a spirit of apology and repentance. In the short term, sharing this information with your spouse may be difficult, but in the long run, it will be better for your marriage to have honesty and transparency. It may also be helpful to bring in a third party, such as a pastor or counselor, to help foster communication and rebuild trust.

Seek to cultivate a "secret-free marriage" where you can tell your spouse everything and in which there are no hidden conversations or secret relationships. Maybe this means that you both can look at each other's phones without permission. Or perhaps, you share the same computer passwords or track each other's phones. Honesty and open communication are important for the health of your marriage. Even through sin and temptation, there is hope for reconciliation because of Christ.

> **Even through sin and temptation, there is hope for reconciliation because of Christ.**

"Help, I Don't Want to Have Sex with My Spouse."

Heart Issues

You don't desire sex. Maybe it's been a difficult season in marriage. You've been fighting around the clock and have no desire for intimacy. Or maybe you feel disappointed and disillusioned with life. There's nothing explicitly wrong with your relationship with your spouse; you simply have no energy for anything, including sex. Perhaps when you were younger, you craved regular intimacy, but now, you don't. You can't get your mind to disconnect from your to-do list, and sex has become a chore and a burden to you, not a blessing.

A low sex drive can often be attributed to emotional, relational, or physical factors. At times, a low desire for sex can result from *emotional* distance in your marriage or emotional baggage regarding sex. For example, if you were raised in a "purity culture" environment, you may view sex as bad or dirty. You may believe you can only have sex if there's a purpose, like if you're trying to get pregnant. Even though you are now married, perhaps you haven't been able to "flip the switch" regarding your views about sexuality, and intimacy still feels dirty and wrong. Emotional distance in your marriage or emotional baggage with sex influences your desire for intimacy.

Other times, sex can be the result of *relational* problems. If you have a history of abuse or have experienced consistent selfishness in the bedroom from either your husband or previous partners, this can influence your desire for sex, even years later. Or if you have experienced betrayal, whether in the form of pornography or adultery, the bedroom may not feel like a safe place. It might feel more like a war zone, full of dangers and casualties. Or perhaps sex has become a bargaining chip in your marriage—a reward for good behavior. If your spouse does something well, you reward him with intercourse. If you're unhappy with him, you withhold sex until he is desperate enough to change, even if only temporarily. Sex has become primarily a tool to produce good behavior from your husband. You engage in "duty sex" either as a reward or as a means to keep your husband happy.

04: Purity in Marriage

Finally, your sex drive can also be affected by *physical* factors. Physical or mental conditions, including hormone imbalances, can affect your libido. This can be further aggravated if you don't feel pleasure from sex. Sometimes, pain during intercourse may also arise from medical conditions, such as polycystic ovary syndrome (PCOS) or endometriosis, which require a visit to your doctor's office for diagnosis and treatment. And finally, there may be some seasons in which you and your spouse need to abstain from sex for a certain period of time, such as when you've just given birth. In these cases, it is important to follow your doctor's advice to allow for proper healing and recovery.

Thankfully, through every stressor and tension within your marriage, there is hope. God designed sex as a gift, and His plans are good. Through His Word, He has instructed husbands and wives not to deprive one another sexually. Pending that you do not have medical reasons impacting your sex life, husbands and wives should only abstain from sex for a short, mutually agreed-upon time to focus on prayer (1 Corinthians 7:1–5). God desires husbands and wives to serve one another and enjoy sexual intimacy within the context of marriage. Through every season of life, you can be faithful to the Lord and your husband as you grow in affection for Christ.

Gospel Hope

God Loves You.

If you are in Christ, God is satisfied with you, and He is pleased with you. His love is not conditional, based on your performance or desire for Him. You are loved perfectly and completely. Not only this, but God offers you complete healing and hope in Jesus. His care for you is constant, and His love for you is sufficient.

There is Hope for Your Marriage.

God can bring healing to the emotional, relational, and physical problems underlying your lack of desire. He can change your affections and heal your past wounds. He can bring restoration to your relationship with your husband and renew intimacy within your marriage. The good news is that God did not design sex for only one spouse to enjoy. Biblical books like the Song of Songs help us understand that God designed sex within marriage to be an enjoyable experience for both husbands and wives. While there may be seasons when sex is more enjoyable for one partner or the other, there is hope for intimacy within your marriage because God's design for sex is good. As discussed on page 62, we are called in Scripture to regular times of intimacy in marriage. As we grow as disciples of God, we can also grow in our intimacy out of reverence for God and love for our spouse.

Jesus Is Better.

Even if you never have a satisfying sex life on this earth, God is completely sufficient for complete, all-satisfying joy. We can be content in the Lord because He is enough for us in every season of life, and He has created us for closeness with Him. While sex is one way we can experience tangible pictures of His love, it is not the only way.

One day, sex will be no more, and we will see Christ face to face. Just as two become one in marriage, we will be with God one day, enjoying and loving Him forever. God will satisfy us and fill us with greater joy than we ever imagined. These temporary troubles and trials will end, and we will be with the One our souls love.

Although intimacy problems within marriage can sometimes feel all-consuming, God is greater than every trouble and is enough for you in every season.

Practical Help

Sex is a gift to be enjoyed within marriage. If you are experiencing a low sex drive or are not desiring intimacy with your husband, consider the following practical help:

Evaluate

It is easy to let frustrations in marital intimacy grow without reflecting on any underlying causes. Spend time evaluating areas of stress in your life, whether due to job transitions, busy schedules, or young children. Evaluate your view of sex and any emotional, relational, or physical contributors to a low sex drive. Talk about your conclusions with your spouse.

Pray

Although it may feel strange at first, pray to God about your marital intimacy. God is the Creator of sex, and He designed it for your good. If you are experiencing trouble within your marriage, pray and ask the Lord for help. Pray for a greater desire for your husband and intimacy in your marriage. In every season and through every struggle, go to the Lord and ask for His help.

Talk

Communication is also an important factor in improving intimacy. For women, a desire for sex often grows out of relational closeness. As the saying goes, "Sex begins in the kitchen." In other words, what happens throughout the day-to-day moments of marriage can influence how much women desire sex. Spend time evaluating how you would like your marriage to grow. If there are areas in your marriage where you are dissatisfied, communicate those desires to your spouse in love. For example, if you desire more conversation or help with daily chores, gracefully communicate those requests to your husband. Do not communicate these as a bargaining chip for more sex; rather, communicate them as a means to strengthen the overall intimacy of your marriage. Furthermore, make sure you also communicate what pleases or doesn't please you in the bedroom.

Many women also find it helpful to regularly remember what attracted them to their husbands at the beginning of their relationship and practice daily thankfulness. Use the space below to begin this processing:

What first attracted me to my husband was:

_____

_____

_____

I am thankful for my husband because:

_____

_____

Some of the sweetest moments of our marriage have been when:

_____

_____

_____

I love my husband because:

_____

_____

_____

Listen

Similarly, be a good listener to your spouse. Ask your husband how regularly he would prefer sex, and seek to love your spouse through regular times of intimacy. For many men, regular dismissals of their advances by their wives can become deep wounds of rejection. Thus, at times, there may be seasons when it is helpful to schedule sex as an expression of loving your husband. Scheduling times for sex does not diminish the beauty of sex by not being spontaneous. Rather, it can be a way of honoring your husband when your sex drive is low (1 Corinthians 7:5).

At the same time, the goal is not to make what many call "duty sex" a common occurrence. God designed sex as a gift for both husbands and wives. Therefore, if you do not desire sex, talk with your husband about ways to make the bedroom a safe and enjoyable space for both of you.

Get Help

Sex is often, though not always, a temperature gauge on the health of your marriage. Spend time evaluating any underlying issues, and talk to your spouse about them. However, as previously discussed, it is also important to recognize that there are physical factors and conditions—such as hormone imbalances, PCOS, endometriosis, and others—that may be contributing to a low sex drive and/or pain during sex. This is not an exhaustive list, so it is important that you visit a doctor for proper diagnosis and treatment if you suspect that you may be facing one of these conditions. Similarly, mental health conditions such as anxiety and depression can contribute to a low sex drive, so it may be helpful to visit a counselor, too. Both doctors and counselors can be incredibly helpful resources for those whose low sex drive may be the result of physical or mental factors.

"Help, I Have a Greater Sex Drive than My Husband."

Heart Issues

You feel rejected and crushed. Your husband doesn't desire intimacy as often as you do. In the quiet moments of the night, you wonder, *Why doesn't he want me? Does he not love me? Aren't men supposed to have a higher sex drive than women?* These thoughts make you feel anxious and insecure, thinking, *Does he not find me beautiful? Is my husband satisfying his sexual desire with someone else?* You feel a deep longing for sex with your spouse, consistently desiring more intimacy but consistently disappointed.

Within marriage, it is normal for one spouse to have a higher sex drive than the other. Although men often stereotypically have a stronger sex drive than women, this is not always the case. At times, wives can experience a greater sex drive than their husbands. The difference in sexual drive in marriage can often cause conflict, as unmet desires and uncommunicated expectations fuel bitterness and division. Not only this, but a lack of intimacy within the bedroom can also breed a lack of intimacy and conflict in other areas of marriage. When you feel hurt or disappointed in the bedroom, you begin to withdraw from your husband throughout the day as well.

Even if there is tension in your marriage within the bedroom, there is still hope. God is sufficient for your every need and desire, and He will help you. He has provided everything you need for faithful obedience and joy in this life. God will never abandon you, and He is your greatest joy.

Gospel Hope

Your Hope Is Secure in Christ.

Your joy in life is not dependent on a satisfying sex life. It is rooted in Christ alone. Even when other areas of your life leave much to be desired, you can find complete joy and fulfillment in Christ. Even when your husband's sexual rejection makes you feel undesirable, there is hope for you because God loves you, and His love is sufficient. He calls you lovely, beautiful, and desirable in Christ. You have all you need.

> *Your joy in life is not dependent on a satisfying sex life. It is rooted in Christ alone.*

By the Spirit's power, you can grow in self-control and love for your spouse. God can redeem even the deepest conflicts or disagreements in marriage because God designed sex for the enjoyment of husbands and wives within marriage. Yet even if you never experience sexual satisfaction on earth, you can still live a fulfilled life in Christ.

Growth in Intimacy Is Possible.

Additionally, there is hope for growth in your marital intimacy. In marriage, we are called to love and serve one another out of reverence for Christ. Jesus modeled this for us firsthand on the cross. Though He was fully God, Jesus laid down His life out of love for us, even when we did not deserve His affection. In the same way, we are called to love our husbands, even when they don't deserve it and even when they disappoint us. We can honor our husbands, even when we are not fully satisfied with them, because Christ is enough for us. Our commitment to our spouses is not dependent on their performance or fulfillment of us. It is rooted in the gospel, which never changes and equips us for every good work. God has saved us, and He loves us. In response, we are to be a reflection of God's love to our husbands.

Although it may be tempting to give up any expectation that you will be sexually satisfied in marriage, God desires that your marriage points to the fulfilling beauty of Christ. Even in the darkest of seasons, there is always hope for change because of God's sufficient power. Through communication, counseling, and growth, it is possible to create a marriage that is full of love and joy.

God may allow you to go through seasons of unfulfilled longings, but He will never leave or abandon you. Our unfulfilled longings remind us that God is better than any earthly blessing. Knowing Him is our greatest calling and satisfaction. One day, we will be with Him face-to-face. He is good, and He is enough for us.

Practical Help

If you have a greater sex drive than your husband, it may be tempting to take things into your own hands, either through self-pleasure or manipulation. Yet, in every season, it is important to practice self-control and love. We are to look to the well-being of others above ourselves in all areas of our lives. As it relates to sex within marriage, we are to seek first to honor and serve our spouses. However, it is also essential to communicate our desires to our spouses with gentleness, consistency, and love.

Good communication is important in marriage. If you are unsatisfied with the frequency of sex within your marriage, talk to your husband. Express your desire for increased intimacy and how its lack affects you emotionally. If he does not listen or does not understand the significance of your requests, it may be helpful to see a marriage counselor who can serve as a trusted third party to help you work through conversations about intimacy. It may also be helpful to gently suggest that your husband visit a doctor. Some medical conditions can cause a low sex drive in males.

God has created sex as a gift, and it is okay to ask your husband for a greater frequency of intimacy. Yet, in every area, we are to surrender our desires to the Lord, recognizing that we may be asked to practice self-control out of reverence for Christ. He is worth every act of love, self-control, and gentleness.

OUR UNFULFILLED LONGINGS
REMIND US THAT

God is better than any earthly blessing.

Gospel Hope for Sexual Sin and Brokenness

CHAPTER FIVE

Abuse

IN THIS CHAPTER ────────────────

"*Help, I've Been Abused.*"

While abuse is traumatic and life-changing, there is hope.

05: *Abuse* / 71

05 / Abuse

"Help, I've Been Abused."

The Problem and Statistics

The numbers are devastating. According to the World Health Organization, one in three women has experienced physical and/or sexual violence in their lifetimes. While most of these cases are in the form of intimate partner abuse, domestic violence is not the only form of abuse. Abuse by a friend, relative, or stranger is also very common. Additionally, physical or sexual abuse can also come with emotional and spiritual abuse* as an oppressor tries to assert power over another in multiple areas of life.

For many, these numbers are not just statistics. It's their life. If this is your story, the pain of physical abuse likely haunts your dreams and memories. The memories and trauma of the past likely bring unpredictable fear and panic attacks. If you have a history of abuse, it will also affect your marriage, even if the abuse was years ago. Perhaps a physical move that your husband makes reminds you of your abuser. Or maybe certain seasons of the year or sounds outside remind you of the trauma. On a regular basis, you may experience unexplainable distrust and emotional walls with trouble enjoying intimacy and irrational fear.

You can find freedom and healing in Christ.

While abuse is traumatic and life-changing, there is hope. It is important to note that this booklet could never cover every possible element of abuse. While these biblical principles apply across a wide spectrum of circumstances, your story has many unique details. For help working through the specific details of your story, please find a local trusted biblical counselor or trauma therapist. Over time, with the help of counseling and the Spirit of God, you can find freedom and healing in Christ. While your abuser has taken much from you, he or she did not take your future. He or she did not take the hope, freedom, and grace you have in Christ. God loves you, and He is kinder, better, and more powerful than any abuser. He alone offers you new hope and new life—freedom and a future.

Darby Strickland from The Christian Counseling Educational Foundation (CCEF) defines emotional abuse as a "pattern of behavior which promotes a destructive sense of fear, obligation, shame or guilt." It is an oppressive and manipulative attempt at control that belittles the other, often containing elements of threats, domination, and assertions of power. Similarly, she also defines spiritual abuse as follows: "When control and domination are established by using Scripture, doctrine, or one's 'leadership role' as weapons." This might look like using Scripture to shame or control with power-hungry domination instead of servant-hearted humility. These forms of abuse often make abuse victims feel isolated, ashamed, fearful, crushed, and even physically ill.

Gospel Hope

If you have been abused, it is easy to think that God has abandoned you. *Why did God allow such a horrific event to occur? Couldn't He have stopped it? Isn't He all-powerful? Isn't He loving and good?* While this section on gospel hope is true and life-giving, it may take time for these truths to solidify and produce transformative, palpable peace. Continue to talk through your beliefs, fears, and doubts with a biblical counselor as you remember the following:

God Loves You.

God sees your suffering, and He cares for you. Jesus has never abandoned you, but He is with you through every sorrow. As a Christian, you are God's precious child, holy and beloved. He loves you so much that He came to earth to rescue you from the eternal condemnation of sin, suffering a gruesome death to bring you eternal hope. Not only this, but He knows what it means to experience abuse, having been beaten, verbally abused, and murdered as a man on earth. He understands your pain and is with you in your grief. He loves you, and He cares for you.

Abuse Is Sin.

God does not condone what happened to you. Rather, it is detestable in His eyes. He does not want you to be abused, and He grieves the devastation and destruction of sin. When God made the world, He made it without abuse. He is the author of every good thing, but because of sin, horrible injustices taint God's good world. We don't know why God allows specific horrors to happen, but God will not allow evil to have the final say in our lives. He promises to redeem every hurt and somehow use it for our good (Romans 8:28).

Abuse Is Never Your Fault.

Even if your body responded with pleasure to the abuse, it is not your fault. Even if you wore a provocative outfit or were out late at night, it is not your fault. Abuse is never your fault. Abuse is the sin of your abuser, and he or she alone bears the weight of judgment for that sin before God. You did nothing to deserve abuse. God condemns abuse, and He is the righteous judge who will one day bring perfect justice to the world.

Note: Even if you know the abuse is not your fault, you may still feel ashamed, dirty, or worthless because of your abuse. See the "Gospel Hope for Sin and Shame" section on page 34, and continue talking with your counselor about the application of these ideas. Christ sets you free from shame, and He will bring healing for every hurt. One day, He will make everything right again.

> **God will not allow evil to have the final say in our lives.**

Practical Help

Get to a Safe Space.

If you are currently in danger, get to a safe space with your children if you have any. If you do not know how to get to a safe place, contact 911 or the National Domestic Violence Hotline at 800-799-7233 for immediate help. The National Domestic Violence Hotline is a twenty-four-hour resource that helps women in dangerous situations. (If you live outside of the United States, your country may have similar crisis lines and resources available.)

Cry out to God.

God is your refuge, your very present help in danger. He is always with you, and He is always kind, loving, and faithful. He sees your suffering, and He cares about your safety. You can always talk to God when you are scared or hurt, angry or confused. You can talk to Him when you don't know what to do or are afraid to take the next step. He always listens, always helps, and always protects.

> *God is with you always, and He is your very present help in time of need.*

The Bible is filled with raw prayers from real people who poured out their hearts to God. They shared their feelings of abandonment, their fears, and their doubts. In the same way, cry out to the Lord in your fear, anger, hurt, and despair. Draw near to Him as your help and your support. Tell Him about your fears, and ask for His help for safety and healing. God is with you always, and He is your very present help in time of need (Psalm 46:1).

Talk to the Police and/or Social Services.

If you have been abused, get help as soon as possible. Talk to the police and/or social services, and bring any evidence you have, such as clothing with DNA. If you are currently in danger, make sure that you and your children are in a safe place. Even if your abuse happened years ago, talking to the police may provide closure for you and protect other victims from also being abused.

Talk to Your Husband.

If you haven't already, communicate with your husband about what has happened. Abuse can often affect current intimacy within your marriage, as trauma and triggers can bring to mind negative memories and associations with sex. As you can, talk with your husband about how past abuse may affect you. Are there moments when you feel especially triggered? Do intrusive thoughts invade at particular times? Because of the sensitivity of this topic, it will be helpful to include a third-party counselor who can help you and your husband understand the impact of the abuse.

What if Your Husband Is Your Abuser?

If your husband is your abuser, get to a safe place before calling the police. Create a safety plan and contact social services or a women's shelter for additional help. Ask your church and social services for help to address any immediate needs, such as transportation, legal advice, financial help, childcare, and medical care. In cases of current abuse, you will need to act quickly with wisdom and tact to protect yourself and your children, if you have any.

Many women don't talk to others about their abuse because they fear no one will believe them. Maybe your husband is charismatic, outgoing, and kind, while the years of abuse have brought out a harsher, meaner side of you in public. You're afraid that everyone will think you're the problem, not him. Or maybe you are scared of being judged by others or blamed for the abuse. You may also experience codependency issues, where you have wrapped up your identity in your husband and find it difficult to leave, even for your own safety.

God does not want you to submit to, excuse, or ignore abuse, even if your abuser is your husband. God despises abuse of any kind, and if your husband is abusing you, get help as soon as possible. God goes before you, and He will help you.

Talk to Your Pastor, a Counselor, and Trusted Friends.

Your church leaders are God's design to shepherd your soul. If you are currently wrestling with the effects of past or current abuse, talk to your pastors. As you share about your abuse and concerns with your pastors, ask for a woman to also be in the room if that would help you feel more comfortable. Your pastors may be able to help you in tangible and financial ways, as well as by processing the crisis of faith that many abuse victims experience. They can help you with lingering doubts and questions such as, "Is God even real?" or "If God is good, why did He allow this to happen?" Not only this, but they can pray for you and help you with your day-to-day needs.

Sadly, because we live in a broken and fallen world, you may have experienced abuse from the very pastors or church leaders who are supposed to shepherd you. If this is your experience, we recommend that you find a trusted biblical counselor and a support group to help you process the effects of abuse.

What's more, counselors and support groups are not only helpful for those who have suffered abuse under pastors or church leaders—they can be a helpful resource for anyone who has faced any type of abuse. A biblical counselor can help you work through your internal dialogue and beliefs—such as *I'm worthless, I deserved this,* or *I'm not worthy of real love*—while reminding you of God's eternal love for you. Additionally, a biblical counselor, especially one with trauma training, can help you process deeper heart emotions and discuss intimacy within your present marriage.

Finally, as you seek help from professionals, find safe, trusted friends within your local church who can encourage you with the truth of God's Word, pray for you, and be a stable source of friendship.

"

God despises abuse of any kind.

CHAPTER SIX

Homosexuality and Transgenderism

IN THIS CHAPTER ───────────

"Help, I'm Attracted to Someone of the Same Sex."
"Help, I'm Questioning My Gender Identity."

Through every form of sexual temptation,

God has provided a way of escape for you

so that you will not fall.

06 / Homosexuality and Transgenderism

"Help, I'm Attracted to Someone of the Same Sex."

Heart Issues

You've been married for some time yet still feel sexually attracted to women. Maybe you thought that being married to a man would remove these desires. Or maybe, for as long as you can remember, you've always been attracted to both men and women. Or perhaps it's a new sensation for you to desire a woman sexually. In any case, you find yourself currently attracted to someone of the same sex. Depending on your cultural context, you might feel additional shame for this attraction that keeps you from talking to anyone else about your feelings. Yet while your thoughts may remain hidden from others, they regularly consume your mind and fill you with confusion and guilt.

Because of the Fall, we all experience temptation. Due to the sin and brokenness of the world, a wedding ring does not guarantee emotional or physical fidelity. Not only this, but our sexual desires have been distorted by sin. For some married women, this looks like lusting after a man who isn't their spouse. For others, it means lusting after another woman. Both forms of lust bring division, hurt, and feelings of betrayal to marriages.

As we discuss this topic, it is important to note that your lust for another woman does not place you beyond the hope of God's grace. Rather, through every form of sexual temptation, God has provided a way of escape for you so that you will not fall (1 Corinthians 10:13). He can help you not only bring your temptations into the light but also stand firm on the Word of God. It may also be helpful to read the section titled "Help, I'm Attracted to Someone Who Isn't My Spouse" on page 54. Many of the principles mentioned in that section apply to this question as well.

What Does the Bible Have to Say about Same-Sex Attraction?

Have you ever wondered what the Bible has to say about same-sex attraction? Some progressive churches affirm same-sex marriages, while others do not. Some churches promote gender fluidity, while others believe that God created two genders, male and female.

The most important question about this topic is: What does the Bible say? As we have discussed, we learn about God's design for sexuality through His Word (see "God's Design for Sexuality" on page 6). In Scripture, we see that God created man and woman in His image, made in His likeness. He designed sex as a gift to be enjoyed between a man and a woman in marriage.

Scripture is clear that there are many kinds of sexual sin, including same-sex intimacy (Leviticus 18:22, Leviticus 20:13, Romans 1:26–27, 1 Corinthians 6:9). Yet some people use the Bible to say that God supports same-sex relationships. Their argument is that Scripture's condemnation of homosexuality is not a moral condemnation but a cultural one. For example, they say that verses such as Romans 1:26–27 do not condone homosexuality, but rather, they condone forced sexual relationships. They say this because, in Roman culture, wealthy individuals could demand sex with whomever they wanted, including slaves of the same sex. As a result, some modern readers conclude that these verses are not moral commands against same-sex relationships today but rather outdated cultural commands that speak about unequal power dynamics within sex.

In his book *People to be Loved*, Preston Sprinkle addresses these kinds of arguments. Through nine points, he concludes that the Bible is clear on its promotion of heterosexual marriages. We have included his points below for easy reference:

The Bible only affirms heterosexual marriages, including the creation of marriage in Genesis 2.

Jesus highlights sexual differences in marriage in Mark 10:1-12 (i.e., that marriage should be between a man and a woman), even though He didn't have to.

Leviticus 18:22 and 20:13 state in absolute terms that there should be no sexual relations between men and women of the same sex, which is reaffirmed in the New Testament (Romans 1:26-27, 1 Corinthians 6:9-10, 1 Timothy 1:8-11).

There is evidence in Greek and Roman times of consensual relationships between women. Every Jewish writer who wrote about same-sex relations at the time condemned them.

Same-sex marriages are not affirmed in the New Testament.

Jesus did not affirm same-sex relations, nor did His audience contest this from the Scriptures.

Paul's argument in Romans 1 states that same-sex relations are "unnatural." There is no mention of power dynamics, and in context, same-sex relationships among women often included consensual relations.

In 1 Corinthians 6:9, the most common use of the Greek word *arsenokoites* reads, "men who sleep with males," and is likely derived from Leviticus 18:22 and 20:13.

For two thousand years, orthodox Christianity has believed that sex should be between a man and a woman.

While the Scriptures are clear that sex should be between a married man and woman, this can still be a difficult topic to navigate personally. If you are struggling with same-sex attraction, God offers you fullness, satisfaction, and complete love in Himself.

*Much more could be said on this topic. If you are interested in studying this further, consider reading *People to Be Loved* by Preston Sprinkle or *Still Time to Care* by Greg Johnson.

Gospel Hope

God's Grace Is Greater than Your Sins.

If you struggle with same-sex attraction, you may be tempted to think that your lustful sins are worse than the sins of others. You don't want to bring them into the light because of fear and shame. But Jesus does not limit His saving power to socially acceptable sins. He came to save His children from all the sin, shame, and brokenness of this world. He came to save sinners like you (1 Timothy 1:15).

We Have All Sinned.

Because of the Fall, there are many kinds of sexual sins and temptations, many of which have been included in this booklet. Before the Lord, none of us can boast because we all have sinned. We are all sinners, and we all sin sexually. No one has the right to be morally superior to someone else. Even if you have lusted after another woman while married, there is forgiveness and hope available for you in Christ.

We Obey God out of Reverence for Christ.

As Christians, we are all called to live with unfulfilled desires out of reverence for Christ. We should surrender the lusts of the flesh because we love God and want to honor Him. Therefore, even though you experience attraction toward another woman, you do not need to act on your desires. As you work out your salvation with fear and trembling, remember that God is the One who works in you, both to will and to work for His good pleasure (Philippians 2:12–13). He will not leave you, but He will sustain you in your fight against the flesh. Your obedience to God's Word is not only for God's glory but also for your good. Even though you may wrestle against this temptation for the rest of your life, God has given you everything you need to resist sin and honor Him.

> *Your obedience to God's Word is not only for God's glory but also for your good.*

God Loves You.

God is not surprised by your sin or temptation, and He can help you remain faithful to your husband, even when you feel attracted to another woman. He loves you and can sustain you in your marriage. He will provide the grace you need each day.

Practical Help

If you are experiencing same-sex attraction:

Study the Bible to Discover Your Identity in Christ.

Scripture defines your identity, not by your sexuality but by your salvation. Despite what Western culture promotes, you are not "less whole" because you deny your sexual longings. Instead, you are a child of God who is trying to honor your heavenly Father. We are all sinners in need of God's grace, and it will be helpful for you to root your identity in Christ as you resist sexual temptation.

Talk to Your Husband.

It is important to discuss all kinds of temptations and struggles with your spouse, including your attraction to another woman. If you are unsure how to bring up the conversation, consider sharing from a place of humility, taking full responsibility for sinful lust, and asking your husband for help in resisting temptation and making wise decisions.

Do not use this conversation as an opportunity to share your grievances with your husband or blame him for your same-sex attractions. For example, refrain from saying things like, "If only you were a better listener, I wouldn't be tempted in this way." Rather, in a spirit of humility, confess your sins to your husband, being mindful that your husband may respond in a myriad of ways. He may feel insecure, questioning if you are attracted to him. He may feel betrayed, wondering if you've been lying to him from the beginning of your relationship. Or he may feel confused, not understanding what you are trying to tell him.

As you share with your husband, be sensitive to how he processes information, and be mindful to pick a good time and place to begin the conversation. Try to create a safe space for you in your marriage to mutually share about your temptations.

Visit a Biblical Counselor.

For help talking through these topics, find a trusted biblical counselor. A counselor can help you work through the details of your story, including what it would look like to be faithful to the Lord and to your spouse, even if you have sexual desires for another person. Consider visiting a counselor alone, as well as setting up a time for couples counseling. It will be important for you and your husband to continue to work through insecurities, temptations, and hurts as a couple, and a trusted third party can often help facilitate these kinds of conversations.

Find Godly Friends.

Turn to godly friends with whom you can openly share your attractions. We all need community, and bringing our temptations into the light with a group of safe friends is helpful. Pursue community in your local church with people who can help you process your temptations and remain faithful to the Lord. As you seek godly accountability, also try to be a godly friend to someone else in return.

"Help, I'm Questioning My Gender Identity."

Heart Issues

You feel like you're wearing a mask. Externally, you know you're a woman. You have the female parts to prove it. But internally, you feel displaced. Being confined to gender norms makes you feel physically sick. You hate that women are expected to cook, bake, and wear the color pink. You like more stereotypically masculine hobbies and get along better with men. You're not even attracted to your husband anymore. You feel confused and disoriented within your marriage. Over time, you begin to wonder, *Am I really a woman, or was I born into the wrong body?* You feel ashamed and alone, like an outsider in your own body. You condemn yourself, thinking, *Surely, God must be disgusted with me.*

The American Psychiatric Association defines gender dysphoria as the "psychological distress that results from an incongruence between one's sex assigned at birth and one's gender identity." Although gender dysphoria has been seen as a medical condition for years, it has become a cultural norm in the West in recent years. It is no longer societally abnormal to transition from one gender to another but is applauded by many in popular culture in some parts of the world. However, as a Christian, you may still wonder, *Is gender simply a construct? And are there only two genders? How do you know you're a woman, especially if you're experiencing such strong emotions that say otherwise?*

If you are questioning your gender identity, it is important to consider how you determine reality. In other words, who tells you who you are?

- Do your emotions determine your gender? If you feel disconnected from your body, is it possible that you were born as the wrong gender?
- Or does society tell you who you are? If you identify more strongly with masculine societal norms or exhibit more masculine traits, are you a man trapped inside a woman's body?
- Or does the Word of God define your reality?

As Christians, God's Word and the Holy Spirit transform us. In this transformation, we allow Scripture to inform our realities, not modern culture (Romans 12:1–2). We are not to let our emotions, societal norms, or parental pressures define our gender identity. Rather, we are to look to the Word of God to understand how God made us.

According to the Bible, God created only two genders, male and female (Genesis 1:27). God is all-knowing and all-wise, and He does not make mistakes. Similarly, He did not make a mistake when He made you a woman. As difficult as life may feel, God has not abandoned you, and there is great help and hope available for you as you seek Him.

Gospel Hope

Who Is God?

If you are questioning your gender identity, you likely feel as if the ground under you has crumbled. Everything you thought was true seems to have changed. You don't know what to believe or who to trust. But although gender dysphoria can be an extremely difficult source of suffering, God is with you.

God does not change, even when you question or fight against reality. He is stable and secure. He is the Creator of the world and the Author of your story. He loves you so much that He sent His only Son to the world to give you new life. He went through the greatest suffering to redeem His children, and He offers restoration and new life in Himself. God's forgiveness is freely and lavishly available for you in Christ. He is faithful to forgive you for any sinful thoughts, raging anger, and lustful desires on this journey.

Who Are You?

You are more than a sum of body parts. You are made in the image of God, perfectly and wonderfully made. As a human, you have a deeper identity than simply your sexual identification. As a Christian, the gospel also gives you a new and unchanging identity. This identity is not primarily founded on your net worth, marital status, or sexual identification. It is founded in Christ. When you trusted in Jesus, you became a child of God, beloved and known by Him. He is your King, and you are His child. He is the Potter, and you are the clay. He is your future, hope, and purpose. Even though you may question your gender identity, your identity in Christ is stable and secure.

God did not make a mistake when He made you. He formed your chromosomes in the womb, and He can help you understand your gender identity in light of His Word. In Scripture, God never separates one's sex from one's gender. Similarly, God can offer you the grace to conform your mind according to His Word.

Practical Help

Study the Scriptures.

If you are struggling with your gender identity, consider the following:

How do you determine what is true? Look up Romans 12:1-2 and John 14:6, and write your reflections below.

_____
_____
_____

How has Jesus's sacrifice on the cross changed you? Read 1 Peter 2:21 and 2 Peter 3:9 to help you answer this question.

_____
_____
_____

What does the Bible say about gender, sex, and identity? Look up Genesis 1:27, Romans 1:18-32, and 1 Corinthians 13:6, and write down your insights below.

_____
_____
_____

How does Scripture define your identity? Look up Ephesians 1, and write down how the Bible describes your identity in Christ below.

_____
_____
_____
_____

Talk to Your Husband, a Counselor, and Trusted Friends.

It is important to talk to your husband about your gender questioning. Also, find a trusted biblical counselor and godly friends who can remind you of what is true. With the help of your local pastor and/or a biblical counselor, uncover when you started questioning your gender identity and what factors have contributed to this struggle (e.g., strong gender stereotypes growing up).

Set up Godly, Grace-Based Support Systems.

As you seek God's will through the Scriptures, it will take time to reorient your mind according to God's Word and not your emotions or culture. That's okay. Set up strong accountability structures around you, and seek to be faithful to Christ, even through this challenging season. God will never leave you, and as you search His Word, the Spirit will help bring it to mind and remind you of what is true.

> "
>
> **Even though you may question your gender identity, your identity in Christ is stable and secure.**

CHAPTER SEVEN

Difficult Emotions and Sexuality

IN THIS CHAPTER

"Help, I Feel Dirty When My Husband and I Have Sex."
"Help, I Like It When Other Men Notice Me."

You can find freedom in Christ regardless of the source of your past or current shame.

07: Difficult Emotions and Sexuality / 91

07 / Difficult Emotions and Sexuality

"Help, I Feel Dirty When My Husband and I Have Sex."

Heart Issues

You feel dirty. Before marriage, you were taught to ignore your sexual desires. Now, even though you're married, you have difficulty enjoying intimacy with your husband. Sex has become an unhealthy and dutiful exchange with your husband. You may think, *I'll give my body to you for a disconnected moment for your pleasure as long as you leave me alone.* Yet you feel dirty and used.

Often, our feelings of dirtiness regarding sex are the result of past or present shame:

- *Past Shame* - Your current view of sex is often greatly influenced by your upbringing and history with sex. If you grew up during the reign of purity culture, in a time when sex before marriage was elevated as the worst of all sins, you might have a difficult time enjoying sex after you get married. Your brain has been conditioned to view sex as dirty or evil, and it will take time to reorient your thoughts about sex.

    Or maybe due to past trauma, abuse, or the sins of another against you, the gift of sex has been distorted. In your life, sex has been associated with pain and disappointment, not intimacy and pleasure. Or finally, perhaps it is your own sexual sin that haunts you. Even though you know that God has forgiven you for your past sins, you still associate the act of sex as dirty and full of pain.

- *Present Shame* - Maybe it's not your past shame that influences your view of sex. It's your current view of sex. You don't think of sex as a gift from God but a dirty and sensual impulse. This can often result from insecurities, cultural influences, and/or current sin. Your physical insecurities—concerns about the size of your thighs or the amount of your cellulite—make you want to hide. Maybe your husband asks you to do acts that you feel uncomfortable with, and you feel simultaneously uncomfortable and ashamed. You want to please him but feel filthy when you do. Or perhaps the sin of pornography, either by you or your husband, has led to strong feelings of shame within sex.

You can find freedom in Christ regardless of the source of your past or current shame. He offers healing from your past and hope for your future.

Gospel Hope

Sex is a good gift of God to be enjoyed within marriage. But what if you still feel dirty thinking about or engaging in intimacy with your husband? You read verses like 1 Thessalonians 4:3–5 telling Christians to avoid sexual immorality, and you desire to honor God. You don't know how to define sexual immorality and wonder what is "okay" to do with your husband in the bedroom. Thankfully, the Bible speaks to our sexuality. God has the power to transform our minds in accordance with His Word, even as it relates to our sex lives.

What Does the Bible Say about Sex within Marriage?

To the surprise of many Christians, God actually encourages us to enjoy sex within marriage. Proverbs 5:18–19 says, "Let your fountain be blessed, and take pleasure in the wife of your youth. A loving deer, a graceful doe—let her breasts always satisfy you; be lost in her love forever." Not only this, but there is an entire book of the Bible filled with joy in marital intimacy in the Song of Songs. God is not "anti-pleasure." Rather, He designed sex for us to enjoy within the confines of a loving marriage.

Scripture calls us to regular intimacy within marriage and to honor the other spouse. In 1 Corinthians 7:5, Paul tells couples not to deprive one another of sex except for an agreed-upon time to fast and pray. Even the phrase "deprive one another" implies a desire to please the other spouse. While every couple will have different understandings regarding the frequency and specifics of their intimacy together, God designed sex for regular benefit and enjoyment.

It is important to note that within these verses is an exclusive commitment that sex is to be between husband and wife alone. This includes not inviting others into the bedroom physically or electronically, as well as mutually agreed-upon love and care for one another. As it says in Scripture, "Marriage is to be honored by all and the marriage bed kept undefiled, because God will judge the sexually immoral and adulterers" (Hebrews 13:4).

Sex is a gift and is designed to be enjoyed within marriage. God desires for the blessing of sex to be enjoyed within marriage as a picture of His love for us. He sees us completely and loves us fully. God can free you from any shame or brokenness of your past or present. See the section titled "Gospel Hope for Sin and Shame" on page 34 for more about the gospel's transformative power over every form of shame.

Even if you do not experience a satisfying sex life within your marriage, you can still seek to honor your spouse in this area because of your love for God. You can preach the truth of the Scriptures to yourself and follow the Lord's instructions in His Word by growing in regular intimacy with your spouse.

Through it all, remember that Christ is with you. Jesus is enough for you, even if, for a season, intimacy remains a difficult part of your marriage. You can remain faithful to God and obey His Word by growing in your love for God and your husband. The beauty and the power of the gospel affect not only our salvation but also the intimacy we experience in our marriages. Jesus loved us so much that He died for us, and in the same way, we can seek to honor our spouses by growing in this area of our marriages even when it is difficult.

Practical Help

Reflect on Underlying Influences

If you are struggling with feeling like sex is dirty, try to uncover why you feel this way. Is it because of your upbringing or because of past or current shame? Talk with your husband about these reasons and pray to the Lord, asking for His help to create a godly vision for sex. As needed, consider visiting a biblical counselor alone or as a couple to work through this. An outside perspective can be beneficial to help facilitate conversations in your marriage.

Bring Shame to the Light

Shame loves to hide in the dark. If you feel dirty or struggle with intimacy with your husband, talk to your husband and a trusted friend or biblical counselor. Bring your fears, concerns, and shame into the light, knowing that God is the Healer and Author of every good gift. He can grow the intimacy within your marriage and bring healing to past hurts. He covers over every shame.

Prioritize God's Word

As you process the underlying causes of your belief that sex is dirty, train your mind to think about what is true (Philippians 4:8). As women, we often let our emotions define our realities. But instead, we are to transform our minds and interpret our lives according to God's Word. Memorize Scripture that speaks about God's good design for sex. Accept the Lord's forgiveness for any sexual sins from your past while communicating with your husband about any future feelings and concerns. Recognize the Bible's instructions for regular intimacy within marriage, and aim to honor the Lord by growing in this area. If you are engaging in any current sins, such as pornography, bring them into the light through repentance, and receive the Lord's forgiveness afresh each day. His mercies are new every morning; great is His faithfulness (Lamentations 3:23)!

Sex within marriage serves as covenant renewal between spouses, a reminder of the promises you made to one another on your wedding day (Keller). As you are intimate with your husband, you are vulnerable with one another in an act of other-centered love (1 Corinthians 7:1–5). Sex is not only designed for procreation and as a defense against temptation but also for the glory of God. As you retrain your mind to view sexuality according to God's design, remember that God is for you in this. He desires for you to have a biblical understanding of the beauty of sex as you worship Him within your marriage.

> *His mercies are new every morning; great is His faithfulness.*

"Help, I Like It When Other Men Notice Me."

Heart Issues

You want to feel beautiful. You wear provocative clothes, secretly hoping for stolen glances from other men and women. You feel alive and excited when they look at you. The rush of being desired fuels you. It makes you feel giddy and eager for the day.

The desire to feel beautiful, loveable, and attractive is natural. Beauty is from the Lord, and as His image-bearers, we were created in part to bring beauty and order to the world around us. But while this is a natural desire, we can often elevate and distort this craving. We ignore our identity in Christ and instead root our worth in the opinions of others. If other people find us desirable, we feel good about ourselves. If we feel ugly or unattractive to others, we feel crushed. Not only this, but we desire the attention of men who are not our husbands to boost our self-esteem and prove that we are still beautiful. Rather than finding our identities in the unfading beauty of Christ, we root them in the shifting, subjective, and unstable opinions of others.

The Bible tells us that our identity is not based on how we look or what others think about us. Our worth is secure in the Lord. Our Creator makes us beautiful, and we find true beauty by knowing Him. The Bible reminds us of what matters—we don't need anyone else's approval to make us feel alive or excited. Instead, true joy, beauty, and fulfillment come from fearing and loving the Lord (Proverbs 31:30, 1 Peter 3:3–5). Our lives exist to bring Him glory, and in response to His great love, we are to pursue holiness and godliness.

> 66
>
> *Our Creator makes us beautiful, and we find true beauty by knowing Him.*

Gospel Hope

We Are Beloved Because We Are God's Children.

As Christians, our identity is firmly established in God. We are made in God's image, the Beloved One. He has adopted us as His children, and He has lavished us with His forgiveness and grace (Ephesians 1:1–6).

Often, when we desire the attention of other men, we want to feel better about ourselves. We place our worth in being desirable to others, forgetting that we are already fully loved in Christ. Yet God tells us that we have all that we need in Christ. We don't need the approval of others because we have God's approval (Galatians 1:10). In light of this, we are called to focus not on external beauty or affirmation but rather on the inner beauty of faith by trusting in the Lord (1 Peter 3:3–5). While it is okay to take care of our bodies—to paint our nails or wear nice clothes—our beauty is not the source of our hope or worth. Our priorities should be set on cultivating a quiet and gentle spirit, firmly rooted in God, secure and stable in Him.

There Is Beauty in Obeying God.

As a result of God's grace, we are called to glorify God with our bodies (1 Corinthians 6:19–20). This means that we are to put on righteousness and God-honoring deeds in faith and reverence to Him. One way the women of the Old Testament adorned themselves with beauty was through their reverent love of the Lord and submission to their husbands (1 Peter 3:1–5). Scripture calls us to do the same.

Another way we can honor God is by being mindful of what we wear and how we treat others. This means not dressing in a way that intentionally tempts someone else to sin. To be clear, we are each responsible for our own sins. If someone lusts after you, they are fully responsible for their sin before the Lord. At the same time, we should not intentionally lead our brothers or sisters to sin. We can be mindful of what we wear, say, and how we act as an act of serving others (Hill).

Beauty Is Found in Fear of the Lord.

Scripture reminds us plainly that "charm is deceptive, and beauty is fleeting, but a woman who fears the Lord will be praised" (Proverbs 31:30). The Lord looks not to the external appearances but at the heart (1 Samuel 16:7). In this way, let us not be deceived by the culture into believing that our identities are rooted in our bodies or our sexuality. Our identities are firmly rooted in the Lord.

> *Our identities are firmly rooted in the Lord.*

Practical Help

As you seek to bring all of your life under the power of God's Word, prayerfully take the following actions steps:

Evaluate Your Motives.

Why do you want other men or women to look at you? What do you desire for them to give you? Is it self-esteem or a rush of excitement? Are you seeking purpose or significance?

_____
_____
_____
_____
_____

After you have discovered your underlying desires, consider instead: where should you be looking to fulfill these desires?

_____
_____
_____
_____

Meditate on the Word.

Find Scripture that speaks to your motives for attention and reminds you of the hope of the gospel. Identity Bible verses that remind you of true God-honoring beauty. (Sample Scriptures include 1 Samuel 16:7, 1 Peter 3:3-5, and Proverbs 31:30.)

_____
_____
_____
_____
_____
_____

Talk to Your Husband, a Counselor, and a Trusted Friend.

In Scripture, God tells us to confess our sins to one another and pray for one another so that we may be healed (James 5:16). If you desire the lustful attention of a man who is not your husband, confess this to your husband and a trusted friend. As you share with a trusted few individuals, ask for prayers and accountability. Bring any sinful desire into the light, and find hope in Christ's complete forgiveness of your sins (1 John 1:9).

> ❝
> **Bring any sinful desire into the light, and find hope in Christ's complete forgiveness of your sins.**

How Salvation Transforms Our Identity:

Past, Present, and Future

Placing your trust in Christ means your identity is transformed—past, present, and future. We can look at three theological terms—justification, sanctification, and glorification—to better understand the unique ways out identity is shaped as we experience salvation and grow in Christ. As we experience each of these stages, we grow in holiness and become more and more like Christ until the day we are finally made complete in Him.

JUSTIFICATION	SANCTIFICATION	GLORIFICATION
Past*	*Present & Ongoing*	*Future*
Justification is a one-time experience of instant transformation that happens when we put our faith in Jesus Christ. When we are justified, we are made right with God because of the sacrifice of Jesus, and our identity is transformed from sinner to saint.	Sanctification is the process by which our identities become more and more like Christ as we continually grow in Him. Our sanctification is evidence of God's work in our lives. Though the process is slow, we can be confident that God will be faithful to complete it.	Glorification looks forward to the day when Jesus will return to make all things right. We will be physically raised up with Him on the last day—fully cleansed of our sinful natures and free to experience our deepest communion with God for all eternity.
Justification frees us from the **penalty** *of sin.*	*Sanctification frees us from the* **power** *of sin.*	*Glorification frees us from the* **presence** *of sin forever.*
Therefore, if anyone is in Christ, he is a new creation; the old has passed away, and see, the new has come! **2 Corinthians 5:17**	*I am sure of this, that he who started a good work in you will carry it on to completion until the day of Christ Jesus.* **Philippians 1:6**	*Then the righteous will shine like the sun in their Father's kingdom.* **Matthew 13:43a**

It is important to remember that there is nothing we can do to earn any part of our salvation. Our justification, sanctification, and glorification do not happen by our efforts, but they are gifts of grace from God, only made possible by Christ's death on the cross. It is in Him that we find our true identity.

If you have accepted Jesus as your Lord and Savior, your justification was a past event at a specific moment in time. However, if you have never confessed your sins and admitted your need for Christ, this is something you can do right now. The Savior's arms are open.

Will God Forgive Me of My Past Sins?

A Prayer of Repentance from Psalm 51

If you are still struggling with guilt or shame for past sexual sins, cling to Jesus. He forgives you of every sin—past, present, and future. When He saved you, He gave you a new identity. As it says in 1 Corinthians 6:9–11:

> Don't you know that the unrighteous will not inherit God's kingdom? Do not be deceived: No sexually immoral people, idolaters, adulterers, or males who have sex with males, no thieves, greedy people, drunkards, verbally abusive people, or swindlers will inherit God's kingdom. And some of you used to be like this. But you were washed, you were sanctified, you were justified in the name of the Lord Jesus Christ and by the Spirit of our God.

Though we were condemned because of our sins, God has forgiven us in Christ. Jesus paid the penalty for every sin, and He has made us clean and forgiven.

Meditate on the truth of Scripture, and pray the words of David to the Lord, found in Psalm 51:

Be gracious to me, God,
according to your faithful love;
according to your abundant compassion,
blot out my rebellion.
Completely wash away my guilt
and cleanse me from my sin.
For I am conscious of my rebellion,
and my sin is always before me.
Against you—you alone—I have sinned
and done this evil in your sight.
So you are right when you pass sentence;
you are blameless when you judge.
Indeed, I was guilty when I was born;

I was sinful when my mother conceived me.
Surely you desire integrity in the inner self,
and you teach me wisdom deep within.
Purify me with hyssop, and I will be clean;
wash me, and I will be whiter than snow.
Let me hear joy and gladness;
let the bones you have crushed rejoice.
Turn your face away from my sins
and blot out all my guilt.
God, create a clean heart for me
and renew a steadfast spirit within me.
Do not banish me from your presence
or take your Holy Spirit from me.
Restore the joy of your salvation to me,
and sustain me by giving me a willing spirit.
Then I will teach the rebellious your ways,
and sinners will return to you.
Save me from the guilt of bloodshed, God—
God of my salvation—
and my tongue will sing of your righteousness.
Lord, open my lips,
and my mouth will declare your praise.
You do not want a sacrifice, or I would give it;
you are not pleased with a burnt offering.
The sacrifice pleasing to God is a broken spirit.
You will not despise a broken and humbled heart, God.
In your good pleasure, cause Zion to prosper;
build the walls of Jerusalem.
Then you will delight in righteous sacrifices,
whole burnt offerings;
then bulls will be offered on your altar.

Gospel Hope for Sexual Sin and Brokenness

CHAPTER EIGHT

The Hope of the Gospel

IN THIS CHAPTER ────────────────

There is Hope for Your Past.
There is Hope for Your Present.
There is Hope for Your Future.

> There is complete, all-consuming, and absolute hope for you in Christ.

God is the Author and Creator of sex. He is the Good Shepherd, who loves His children, and He designed sex as a gift that points toward His love. Yet, because of the brokenness of the world, the gift of sex is often distorted and manipulated. Pornography, shame, and abuse distort God's good design. Thankfully, God is not content to leave us in our brokenness. He promises to come again to heal us and restore every broken thing. There is hope, not only for your past sexual sin or brokenness but also for your present struggles and future healing. There is complete, all-consuming, and absolute hope for you in Christ.

There is Hope for Your Past.

There is hope for your past sexual brokenness in Christ. On the cross, Jesus paid the penalty for your sin. God no longer holds any of your sins against you. He does not "stiff-arm" you or reject you because of your sexual sins, nor does He condemn you for the lustful wonderings of your past. When you trusted in Jesus for salvation, He cleansed you of every sinful thought, action, and motive. He saved you and brought you into His family.

Though we will continue to struggle with sin in this life, when we do, we can rest in Christ. His finished work has restored us in God's sight. This restoration means that we will be not only freed from our past sin but also healed from any shameful sin that has been inflicted upon us (1 John 1:9, Romans 10:11, Psalm 25, Psalm 69:6). Through Christ, there is wholeness, purity, forgiveness, and grace for your past.

There is Hope for Your Present.

Not only does God forgive you for your past, but He also gives you the hope you need each day. He forgives you, loves you, and supplies all you need in Christ. He equips and empowers you through His Spirit that lives in you. He changes you. But not only this—God is also active with you. Jesus Christ, who was perfect in every way, intercedes for you at the right hand of the Father. You are no longer in bondage to sin or shame, but Christ has given you the Spirit that helps you say "no" to temptation. He is with you, empowering you to resist sin and healing you from sexual hurts that currently haunt you.

There is Hope for Your Future.

One day, there will be no more sin or shame. When Christ comes again, He will replace every hurt with joy and restore every bondage with freedom. He will make right every wrong. There will be no more pornography, divorce, abortions, or abuse. There will be no more sexual brokenness or pain. You will be set free forever from every sin and shame. He will heal every hurt and restore every form of brokenness. He will return at last, and you will finally be with Him face to face.

In heaven, there will be no more sex. You will not be married anymore, and there will be no more marital physical intimacy (Matthew 22:30). Instead, whatever joy and pleasure you once received through sex will seem minuscule compared to the joy you have of being united with your Savior. The momentary gift of sex is designed to point you toward the Savior's love, but one day, you will need the substitute no more. You will be with Jesus face to face, experiencing the fullness of His love forever.

Because of this past, present, and future hope, you can have courage today, even amid great pain and brokenness. Christ is coming again, and He is worthy of our worship. When He returns, He will bring perfect healing, joy, and an all-satisfying love. He will make all things new.

> **The momentary gift of sex is designed to point you toward the Savior's love.**

Revelation 21:1–6

Then I saw a new heaven and a new earth; for the first heaven and the first earth had passed away, and the sea was no more. I also saw the holy city, the new Jerusalem, coming down out of heaven from God, prepared like a bride adorned for her husband. Then I heard a loud voice from the throne: Look, God's dwelling is with humanity, and he will live with them. They will be his peoples, and God himself will be with them and will be their God. He will wipe away every tear from their eyes. Death will be no more; grief, crying, and pain will be no more, because the previous things have passed away. Then the one seated on the throne said, "Look, I am making everything new." He also said, "Write, because these words are faithful and true." Then he said to me, "It is done! I am the Alpha and the Omega, the beginning and the end. I will freely give to the thirsty from the spring of the water of life."

"

Because of this past, present, and future hope, you can have courage today, even amid great pain and brokenness. Christ is coming again, and He is worthy of our worship.

When He returns, He will bring perfect healing, joy, and an all-satisfying love. He will make all things new.

BIBLIOGRAPHY

Chalmers, Thomas. *The Expulsive Power of a New Affection.* Crossway Short Classics. Wheaton, IL: Crossway, 2020.

Chesnut, Ashley. *It's Not Just You: Freeing Women to Talk about Sexual Sin and Fight It Well.* Nashville, Tennessee: B&H Publishing Group, 2021.

Daniels, Kyra. *Worthy: Embracing Your Identity in Christ.* Hanover, MD: The Daily Grace Co.®, 2022.

DeYoung, Kevin. "Worldly Grief." *The Gospel Coalition.* June 1, 2010. https://www.thegospelcoalition.org/blogs/kevin-deyoung/worldly-grief/.

Dickson, Krystal, Chris McKenna, and Shelby Turner. "Pornography Bonus Episode: Protecting Young Eyes." May 12, 2022. In *Daily Grace.* Produced by The Daily Grace Co., 50:59. https://dailygracepodcast.com/episode/pornography-bonus-episode-protecting-young-eyes-with-chris-mckenna/.

Got Questions Ministries. "What is the meaning of the Parable of the Unforgiving / Unmerciful Servant?" *Got Questions.* Accessed May 24, 2022. https://www.gotquestions.org/parable-unforgiving-servant.html.

Groves, Alasdair. "What Should I Tell My Spouse About My Sexual Sin." *CCEF National Conference* 2012. Accessed February 9, 2023. https://www.ccef.org/wp-content/uploads/archive/Breakout%20Outline-%20What%20Should%20I%20Tell%20My%20Spouse%20About%20My%20Sexual%20Sin%20(Groves).pdf.

Groves, Alasdair, and David Powilson. "Gender Identity." February 6, 2017. In *CCEF Podcast: Where Life & Scripture Meet.* Produced by Christian Counseling & Educational Foundation (CCEF). https://ccef.libsyn.com/webpage/2017/02.

Hambrick, Brad. "Seminar: Taking the Journey of Grief with Hope." *Brad Hambrick.* Blog. September 23, 2011. http://bradhambrick.com/grief/.

Hill, Megan. "The Modesty Conversation We Need to Have." *The Gospel Coalition.* June 29, 2021. https://www.thegospelcoalition.org/article/modesty-conversation/.

Hilton, Donald L., and Clark Watts. "Pornography addiction: A neuroscience perspective." *Surgical Neurology International*. February 21, 2011. https://doi.org/10.4103/2152-7806.76977.

Holmes, Jonathan and Deepak Reju. *Rescue Plan: Charting a Course to Restore Prisoners of Pornography*. Phillipsburg, NJ: P&R Publishing Company, 2021.

Holmes, Jonathan and Deepak Reju. *Rescue Skills: Essential Skills for Restoring the Sexually Broken*. Phillipsburg, NJ: P&R Publishing Company, 2021.

Johnson, Greg. *Still Time to Care: What We Can Learn from the Church's Failed Attempt to Cure Homosexuality*. Grand Rapids: Zondervan Reflective, 2021.

Jones, Robert. *Uprooting Anger: Biblical Help for a Common Problem*. Phillipsburg, NJ: P&R Publishing, 2005.

Keller, Timothy, with Kathy Keller. *The Meaning of Marriage: Facing the Complexities of Commitment with the Wisdom of God*. New York: Penguin Books, 2016.

Lewis, C. S. *The Weight of Glory*. New York: Macmillan, 1949.

Madison, Reggie. "What to Do When You Catch Your Husband Watching Porn." *First Things First*. August 13, 2020. https://firstthings.org/husband-watching-porn/.

Merriam-Webster, Inc. *Merriam-Webster's English Dictionary*. Springfield, MA: Merriam-Webster, Inc., 2005.

Online Sunshine. "The 2021 Florida Statutes." Official Internet Site of the Florida Legislature. Accessed February 10, 2023. http://www.leg.state.fl.us/statutes/index.cfm?App_mode=Display_Statute&Search_String=&URL=0700-0799/0741/Sections/0741.28.html.

Owen, John. *The Mortification of Sin: Unabridged*. United States: CreateSpace, 2013.

Porn Hub. "Pornhub Insights: Digging Deep into the Data." Accessed March 23, 2022. https://www.pornhub.com/insights/.

Powlison, David. *How Does Sanctification Work?* Wheaton, IL: Crossway, 2017.

Powlison, David. "How specific should a husband be in confessing lust to his wife?" *Christian Counseling & Educational Foundation (CCEF)*. July 5, 2016. https://www.ccef.org/video/how-specific-should-husband-be-confessing-lust-his-wife/.

Sande, Ken. *The Peacemaker: A Biblical Guide to Resolving Personal Conflict.* Grand Rapids: Baker Book House, 1991.

Simonyi-Gindele, Caleb, and Verlynda Simonyi-Gindele. "How to Confront Your Husband About His Pornography Addiction." April 8, 2022. In *The Marriage Podcast for Smart People*. Produced by OnlyYouForever. 24:44. https://www.onlyyouforever.com/how-to-confront-your-husband-about-his-pornography-addiction/.

Simonyi-Gindele, Caleb, and Verlynda Simonyi-Gindele. "Key Things to Include When Disclosing Infidelity." March 25, 2020. In *The Marriage Podcast for Smart People*. Produced by OnlyYouForever. 27:21. https://www.onlyyouforever.com/key-things-to-include-when-disclosing-infidelity/.

Simonyi-Gindele, Caleb, and Verlynda Simonyi-Gindele. "What To Do When You've Just Discovered Your Husband's Porn Habit." April 12, 2017. In *The Marriage Podcast for Smart People*. Produced by OnlyYouForever. 42:20. https://www.onlyyouforever.com/when-youve-discovered-your-husbands-porn-habit/.

Slattery, Julianna. *Rethinking Sexuality: God's Design and Why It Matters.* New York: Multnomah, 2018.

Sprinkle, Preston. *Embodied: Transgender Identities, the Church, and What the Bible Has to Say.* Colorado Springs: David C Cook, 2021.

Sprinkle, Preston. *People to Be Loved: Why Homosexuality Is Not Just an Issue.* Grand Rapids: Zondervan, 2015.

Sproul, R. C. *The Holiness of God.* Carol Strem, IL: Tyndale House Publishers, 1998.

Strickland, Darby. *Emotionally Abusive Marriages: Restoring the Voice of God to the Oppressed.*" *Christian Counseling & Educational Foundation (CCEF)*, 2016. https://www.ccef.org/wp-content/uploads/2016/02/Emotionally-Abusive-Marriages-FINAL-1.pdf.

Thorne, Helen. *Purity Is Possible: How to Live Free of the Fantasy Trap*. Epsom: The Good Book Company, 2014.

Treasures. "Our Work." *I Am Treasures Website*. Accessed May 20, 2022. https://www.iamatreasure.com/our-work.

Truman, Jennifer L., and Rachel E. Morgan. "Nonfatal Domestic Violence, 2003-2012." *U.S. Department of Justice*. April 2014. https://bjs.ojp.gov/content/pub/pdf/ndv0312.pdf.

Turban, Jack, ed. "What is Gender Dysphoria?" *American Psychiatric Association*. August 2022. https://www.psychiatry.org/patients-families/gender-dysphoria/what-is-gender-dysphoria.

Welch, Ed. "'Disclose or Be Exposed." *Christian Counseling & Educational Foundation (CCEF)*. July 5, 2012. https://www.ccef.org/disclose-or-be-exposed/.

Welch, Edward T. *Shame Interrupted: How God Lifts the Pain of Worthlessness and Rejection*. Greensboro, NC: New Growth Press, 2012.

Wheeler, Brad. "Does Pornography Use Ever Justify Church Discipline?" *9Marks*. October 30, 2018. https://www.9marks.org/article/does-pornography-use-ever-justify-church-discipline/.

World Health Organization. "Violence Against Women." *The World Health Organization*. March 9, 2021. https://www.who.int/news-room/factsheets/detail/violence-against-women.

Thank you for studying God's Word with us!

CONNECT WITH US
@thedailygraceco
@dailygracepodcast

CONTACT US
info@thedailygraceco.com

SHARE
#thedailygraceco

VISIT US ONLINE
www.thedailygraceco.com

MORE DAILY GRACE
The Daily Grace® App
Daily Grace® Podcast